BECOME A WINNER WITH
IMPACT

On or offstage, in or out of the office, here's the book that can put you on your feet and help you go for the gold!

Gain confidence as you learn how to prepare, analyze, organize, visualize, and deliver a speech like a pro. Here are easy, effective step-by-step techniques, exercises, and examples that can help you discover your own greatest strengths and build on them to become a dynamic, persuasive public speaker. Take a giant step in your career and in your private life as you reap the benefits of your newfound confidence and skill. Discover the book that will help you realize your potential—today!

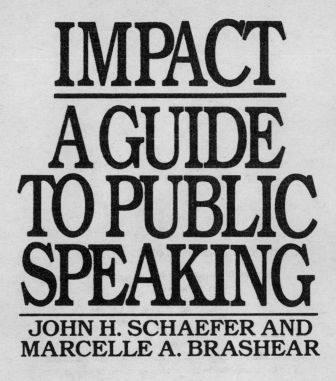

IMPACT

A GUIDE TO PUBLIC SPEAKING

JOHN H. SCHAEFER AND MARCELLE A. BRASHEAR

BERKLEY BOOKS, NEW YORK

IMPACT: A GUIDE TO PUBLIC SPEAKING

A Berkley Book/published by arrangement with
the authors

PRINTING HISTORY
Berkley edition/August 1989

ISBN: 0-425-11691-3

A BERKLEY BOOK ® TM 757,375
Berkley Books are published by The Berkley Publishing Group
200 Madison Avenue, New York, N.Y. 10016.
The name ''BERKLEY'' and the ''B'' logo
are trademarks belonging to Berkley Publishing Corporation.

PRINTED IN THE UNITED STATES OF AMERICA

10 9 8 7 6 5 4 3 2 1

Contents

IMPACT

A GUIDE TO PUBLIC SPEAKING

INTRODUCTION

In a *Book of Lists* survey, Americans were asked to name their most intense fear. Surprisingly enough, the most common answer was not fire, heights, bugs, or even death. The number-one fear of those surveyed is public speaking. Now, human nature being what it is, we don't usually like to do something of which we are downright terrified. So why are we willing to subject ourselves to the trauma of standing up in front of people and trying to say something that makes sense?

Our hearts pound and our stomachs feel like we're on a roller coaster. Our legs freeze up when we want to move and shake when we want to stand still. Our hands are so sweaty we can't possibly keep hold of a microphone, and if we're lucky, our voices only go up one octave when we speak.

With all this to deal with, there have to be some pretty good reasons why we choose to work toward becoming better speakers. Well, one obvious reason is that good speaking skills will help your career. There's nothing like face-to-face communication to get a message across: if you are communicating on behalf of your employer, you are making yourself a valuable employee; if you are communicating on your own behalf, you are more likely to achieve your personal objectives.

People who speak well at meetings and in front of groups are seen as more professional, and that certainly can't hurt. And who knows? Being a good communicator may be just what gets you into the deal you want on the new car you are buying, and out of a boring dinner engagement!

But there are more important reasons for overcoming the fear of public speaking than what it will do for your career or your pocketbook. And that is what it will do for you.

There is something about learning to communicate well that changes how you see and feel about yourself. One of the greatest rewards for communication trainers is that we have the opportunity to see this change take place almost right in front of our eyes.

Time and again people who can barely get through their first presentation enroll in speaking classes only to look like pros by the end of the course. And it isn't because they are taught some magic formula. It's because they have learned to focus on their strengths as a speaker and build, one step at a time, on what they can already do.

You will experience this growth in skills and confidence too. All you need are two basic ingredients: a good perception of reality and a good imagination.

You need a good perception of reality so that you can identify your strengths as a speaker. What are you especially good at? Do you have good eye contact? A strong voice? Maybe you have a flair for developing great visual aids or are comfortable using gestures. Discover what you do well, and then remind yourself of your strengths every time you begin to speak. That will help you gain the confidence you need to begin improving in other areas.

Next you need your imagination. Envision yourself as the best speaker you can imagine. Visualize yourself in a full-house auditorium going through a presentation from start to finish—the way you wish you could.

Keep this image on file in your mind and play it back every time you are getting ready to give a talk. Be aware of both where you are in reality and what your ideal image is. Then, one step at a time, work toward that image.

It's not unlike the concept of a self-fulfilling prophecy, a term that means the prediction of events that do, in fact, happen because the prediction is the cause.

Many athletes use a similar technique, imagining the race or competition ahead of time and visualizing every moment of it—including a victorious finish. Jack Nicklaus, professional golfer, once said, "I never hit a shot, not even in practice, without having a very sharp, in-focus picture of it in my head."

Another example of this approach is the children's book *The Little Engine That Could*. This simple story is about a small train engine that is given the task of pulling a very great load up a huge mountain. The engine's first attempts fail, but he finally makes it by saying to himself, over and over again, "I think I can, I think I can, I think I can."

Becoming an effective speaker is not very much different from what that little engine did. *Thinking you can* is developing the right mental attitude toward public speaking. It does wonders for your self-confidence, and it's so much fun to see yourself become more and more like your vision.

This is the positive change you will experience in how you see yourself and how you feel about yourself. Mastering the technique of preparing and delivering a good presentation helps you see yourself as a success because you have accomplished something you never thought you would be able to do.

But besides having this wonderful vision of yourself as a speaker, what techniques can you use to gain the skills to help you accomplish the vision? This is what you will discover in *Impact: A Guide to Public Speaking*.

Chapter 1

GAINING CONFIDENCE

The value of an idea is incalculable. Many of our greatest human accomplishments and business enterprises are little more than the fulfillment of a single idea. Yet until an idea is communicated, it remains locked up inside the mind; it has no life, no power. The communication of ideas is the source of new knowledge—of change, humor, art—of new ways of doing and being.

The primary purpose of presenting an idea is to share information or motivate people to take action. Your purpose may be to provide information on a new topic; update an audience's current knowledge on a subject; ask that audience to do something specific; or ask it for a contribution. *Impact* will assist you in successfully preparing for and delivering presentations that will accomplish these purposes.

What is a Speech?

Some years ago a well-known humorist and speech critic wrote an article about the "Lost Art of Oratory." He complained that America no longer had orators as great as those of the eighteenth and nineteenth centuries, and that because twentieth-century speakers lacked this oratorical ability, the quality of speaking was deteriorating. He longed for the Patrick Henrys, Daniel Websters, and William Jennings Bryans of the past—the orator with a booming voice, dramatic display, exaggerated gestures, and acting talent.

There was a place for this kind of oratory in the days when large outdoor audiences came to hear a speaker because he or she was a primary source of news; they wanted an entertaining and unusual event. And because listeners didn't have a broad base of information, they expected speakers to "talk down" to them.

What the humorist and critic failed to recognize is a fundamental difference in today's society from that of past centuries: Audiences are more sophisticated and have greater access to information. In many cases, the audience is already very familiar with the topic of the speech. They want to feel that the speaker respects this knowledge and is talking things over with them, rather than preaching to them.

A speech is most often *not* a dramatic performance. Except in rare instances, you are not acting a part; you are always yourself. The more your listeners sense that you are acting a role, the less they will respond to what you say.

A speech is not a public reading. This misconception is advanced by those who deliver a speech by reading words in a monotone from a printed page, usually with their noses buried in the manuscript.

A speech is not a well-practiced set of external mannerisms. The mistake that too many make is to believe that one can become a good speaker just by refining the use of voice, diction, gestures, and props. In reality, effective speaking starts from within you, from the sincere desire to communicate a message to others. Add to this an attitude of respect for your listeners—an appreciation of their beliefs and feelings. An effective speech is talking things over with the listeners in a sincere, enthusiastic manner. The late Eric Johnston, former president of the Chamber of Commerce of the United States and chief spokesperson for the motion-picture industry, was a speaker with rare charm and personal effectiveness. He summed it up this way: "A speech is conversing with your audience as though you were in individual conversation with each member privately."

"Nothing to Fear"

President Franklin D. Roosevelt, in his First Inaugural Address, said that "the only thing we have to fear is fear itself." Although he wasn't talking about public speaking, the quote is a perfect expression of the feelings of almost all speakers, no matter how experienced. Especially if you are a beginning speaker, you might have exaggerated fears of failure and defeat because you aren't sure just what's expected of you.

It's very easy to believe that the audience is supercritical and overrate the possibility of audience hostility. If you are unfamiliar with proven preparation techniques, you'll have a difficult time feeling confident about your speech. This can cause you to doubt the power of your message to command respect and make you underrate the value of what you have to say.

These insecurities are the psychological factors that can break down your morale and create a vicious circle of self-doubt and ineffectiveness. The less confident you are, the less dynamic you will be; the less dynamic you feel, the less confidence you will have.

The inexperienced speaker is plagued by questions that even further undermine self-confidence and make it difficult to prepare adequately and present effectively:

• Can I trust myself to remember?

• Do I have anything to say that's worth saying?

• Are they interested in my subject?

• Have I arranged my material in the best way?

Questions like these start you thinking about yourself instead of your message. They make you think of the audience as noticing every little nervous mannerism and critically smiling to themselves. These psychological factors produce a state of mental chaos that not only exhibits itself in physical chaos but also undermines self-confidence and self-respect, destroys your natural charm, and creates such internal confusion that your presentation loses most of its impact.

What can you do about this? How can you break this circle?

As a starting point, understand and accept that stage fright, physical and mental, is practically universal; every speaker has it to some degree. It's not only natural, it's nature's way of preparing you for the occasion with an abundance of "nervous activity."

Every speaker wants to make a good impression on the audience. It's natural to be concerned about the image you project as a speaker and as an individual. Even experienced speakers are subject to this kind of insecurity. Once you begin to look for and find ways to deal with your concerns, your fears will subside. You'll begin to gain confidence in your ability, and speechmaking will not seem so overwhelming a feat. Remember:

- The audience is not against you.

- The audience wants to enjoy themselves—they will get no pleasure out of your misery.

- The audience is not going to be nearly as critical as you think.

- If you are pleasant, the audience will meet you more than halfway.

- If you have something to say about things they are interested in, or present some new and clever way of throwing light on old things, your audience will receive you with open arms.

Controlling Nervousness

The problem of nervousness is one not of elimination but of control. In fact, all this nervous energy is as much an asset as a liability. A certain amount of nervousness is necessary and indispensable; it tunes you up and gives you the extra energy you need to do a good job. The speaker who is free from any nervousness whatsoever may appear insincere and indifferent.

Effective speakers have, through practice, mastered the art of concealing nervousness from the audience by making it work *for* them rather than *against* them. As noted above, the first essential in the control of nervousness is to realize that the audience is usually receptive and uncritical of your speaking style. They gather to listen to you, not to criticize you.

The second essential is to be adequately prepared. Make certain that your analysis has been thorough, your plan of presentation persuasive, and your material appropriate for the occasion. Think only of what you are going to say, and prepare so thoroughly that you can feel confident that you know what you are talking about and that what you are saying is worth standing up for.

The third essential is to master the physical mechanism of your body so that when you face the audience, your nervousness will not show. Most speakers, particularly at the beginning of the presentation, show nervousness by excessive movement of their hands and feet, shifting their body weight back and forth, handling the platform furniture, or other distracting habits.

Some speakers try to relax by smoking during a presentation. Although this might help you breathe deeply, it doesn't do much for your professional image. Listeners view smoking as an expression of nervousness, so avoid this habit while you are speaking. Similarly, don't drink any alcoholic beverages either before or during your talk. Again, this not only displays nervousness, but alcohol will reduce the energy level you need to be effective.

Let your natural energy be the charge you need to speak; don't overdo it with caffeine or sugar, and give your stomach a break—don't eat spicy or heavy meals before you go on. Get plenty of rest the night before you speak. Be kind to your body and it will see you through your presentation with flying colors.

Learning to Relax

The best thing you can do to avoid showing nervousness is to relax. Remember that too much muscle tension is responsible for the quick, awkward, nervous jerks and starts. Learn to control your physical being by practicing relaxation.

Your tensions are not only physical effects of fear; they are also, in part, the cause of fear. To some extent, you're not tense because you're afraid; you're afraid because you're tense. You may tremble because you're frightened, then become more frightened because you tremble. Again, in a stressful situation, nature impels you to breathe at an abnormally fast rate; then, becoming aware of your fast breathing, you breathe even faster. If unchecked, the pressures mount and the result is chaos.

Once you begin to learn to relax, you take a big step toward reducing your nervousness. You'll actually have many opportunities to indulge in relaxation techniques both before and during your presentation. These actions will help you relax, reduce your tension, and will consume some of the surplus energy nature has provided. The key is to channel your nervousness into intentional, constructive motions. Some techniques you can use to reduce muscle tension follow.

Be aware of your body. For most speakers, nervous energy almost always expresses itself in the same way. Notice what your body does to burn excess energy: Do you shuffle your feet, clench your hands, bob your head, or shrug your shoulders? Notice where your nervous energy goes, and work on relaxing those muscles; do that by tensing and releasing them a number of times before you speak.

Relax. Before going forward to speak, relax in your seat. Completely relax the muscles of your arms, legs, neck, torso, and jaw. Slouch in your seat a little if necessary, giving your body a comfortable muscle tone.

Walk slowly. When you walk to the platform, try to relax; force yourself to walk at an easy pace, and resist the inner pressure to rush forward.

Maintain a comfortable stance. When you reach the platform, take a moment to assume a comfortable stance. Sometimes it's helpful to provide for muscle movements that relieve tenseness. You might pick up a book you plan to quote from, arrange the notes your statistics are recorded on, walk to the blackboard and write on it, or adjust the light on the lectern. These activities give your muscles something to do, and lessen their rigidity.

Control your body. While speaking, you might suddenly feel muscle tension in your legs, arms, or neck. This is a good time to tighten those muscles as much as you can, then slowly release the tension. Your audience won't see this, but they will see that you appear more relaxed afterward. These muscle exercises can be even more effective if you follow them by taking a few steps, using a gesture or sweeping your eyes over the entire room to allow your neck to move. Do this anytime you feel physically out of control—tense, then release and use those muscles.

In addition to reducing muscle tension, there are many things you can do to reduce a rapid breathing rate.

• Before you enter the room, take several slow, deep breaths to fill your lungs with fresh air.

- Just before being called upon to speak, and as you walk forward, breathe deeply and slowly.

- When you reach the speaker's stand, pause before you speak to breathe deeply and establish a normal rate of breathing.

- Throughout the speech, pause now and then, not only to organize your ideas but also to give yourself a chance to breathe. Resist the inner pressure to speak too rapidly and breathlessly.

That's all there is to it!

That these techniques really work is attested to by the many speakers who have successfully mastered them and won the battle of reducing the sweaty-palms-and-butterflies syndrome. Just keep in mind that you will never get rid of the butterflies entirely, but you can teach them to fly in formation!

Chapter 2

PREPARATION: AN OVERVIEW

Communication begins with an idea. It may concern something to be built, something to be sold, or a message to be told. However, until this idea is shared with other people, until it is presented, nothing happens. No matter how sound the idea may be, unless it is well presented, it has little chance of success.

The important thing to keep in mind is that the effective presentation of an idea doesn't just happen. Like a beautiful home, it is built from carefully drawn plans that are revised again and again before the hammer hits the nail. In the same way, good preparation and organization of a presentation cannot be overemphasized. Time and again speakers, even polished ones, have failed to accomplish their objective because their presentations were poorly organized.

When Abraham Lincoln delivered his immortal address at Gettysburg, one of the leading journals of the day described it as a great extemporaneous talk, delivered from a few penciled notes scribbled on the back of an envelope during the train ride to Gettysburg.

Yet later historians found many drafts of the Gettysburg Address, several in Lincoln's own handwriting, showing that he had worked for many weeks writing a speech that was to take only four minutes to deliver. Mentor Graham, one of Lincoln's early schoolmasters, once observed: "I have known Lincoln to study for hours the best of three ways to express one idea."

The man preceding the president on the program spoke for over two hours. He used approximately 60,000 words. Lincoln's famous speech contained only 298 words; 192 were one-syllable and 52 were two-syllable. Lincoln's speech, so well-planned, allowed him to be both brief and clear.

You may never have the opportunity to make a Gettysburg Address, but you will certainly feel a lot more comfortable with your audience, and they with you, if you adopt Lincoln's preparation practices.

Subject

The first and most important consideration in preparing any presentation is what you have to say. Choose your topic from among things about which you have an inner excitement, with which you have a personal experience, or of which you have a deep knowledge. It's that irresistible spark of conviction and enthusiasm that most effectively transmits a message; so give yourself the opportunity to be really dynamic! Whenever you stand before an audience to speak, be an "expert." Think in terms of what you do best, and capitalize on those strengths when you give a presentation. And most crucial, unless you're sure you have something new and important to say, perhaps it's better not to say anything at all!

Suppose, however, someone such as your boss asks you to give a presentation on a subject matter you are not familiar with or that is not in your area of expertise. You have a few options.

- Try to decline, perhaps offering the name of another person who can address the subject.

- Offer to speak on a related subject that is within your area of expertise.

- If your boss insists, do a lot of research, interview an expert, prepare thoroughly, and rehearse your answers to possible questions from your audience.

It is unfortunate that we often get stuck giving presentations about unfamiliar material, but when this happens to you, try to find ways to incorporate your own strengths and expertise as much as possible. This may not be one of your best presentations, but it won't be a failure.

Objective

Once you have chosen your subject, you can move on to determining your objective, or what you will achieve through your presentation. The politician's objective is to get the listeners' votes; the advertiser's to persuade the audience to buy a particular product. But not every presentation has an "action" objective. For example, in the talk given to convey information, you may not want your audience to take any specific action. Still, you do have a definite objective: You want your audience to accept an idea.

In any presentation, limit yourself to one simple objective. Otherwise, you'll try to accomplish too much in the allotted time. Consequently, you may end up accomplishing nothing, simply because you tried to convince your audience of too many different ideas in too short a time. Spend considerable thought and time in determining the one clear objective you want to accomplish. It is important, if possible, to talk with the meeting planner or a key member of the audience to mutually determine the objective. Then use this as the foundation for the rest of your talk. After you've determined your objective, everything you say must pertain directly to achieving it.

Strategy

Once you have selected a specific objective, you must plan your strategy.

You are convinced that your objective is sound and your ideas should be accepted by your listeners. However, suppose they hold an opposing opinion, and your task is to persuade them to accept your ideas. This is where strategy comes in. It means planning your approach so that you appeal to the needs, interests, and desires of your listeners. You must put yourself in your listeners' place and decide which of their needs or interests can be related to your idea. Then build your strategy around the fulfillment of these interests. Chapter 3 gives a thorough discussion of the techniques for analyzing your audience's needs.

To communicate effectively, you must be a strategist, psychologist, diplomat, salesperson, and good listener—all in one! But above all else, the effective communicator has empathy—the ability to see and understand the needs of the listener. This quality, complemented by the knowledge of the ways and means to reach the audience with impact, is the stuff of which successful speaking is made.

Organization

The purpose of organization is to arrange your thoughts in a logical sequence for your audience. This makes it possible to hold and build their interest throughout the talk so that when you are finished, they will take whatever action you ask. Following is a simple organization for a talk.

- Get your audience's attention and offer a reason to listen to you.

- State your objective as clearly, fully, briefly, and force-fully as you can. Present your main ideas in an inter-esting way.

- Give facts. Cite examples. If your examples are inter-esting stories, particularly stories involving people, you'll find that your presentation will sparkle. Treat each fact, each example, as a separate package to be dealt with fully before you go on to the next.

- Tell them how they will benefit from your message. What's in it for them to accept your idea?

- Tell your audience exactly what you want them to do. Or, if it is an informational talk, sum up your points concisely and tell them how the information is beneficial to them and how they can apply it.

Chapter 4 provides further discussion of a formula useful for organizing your presentation.

Evaluation

Now evaluate what you have done. Go back and reread your objective. Have you expressed it clearly and early in the talk? Does the main body of your presentation give convincing evidence to support your objective? Have you told your audience what action you want them to take, or what you want them to know?

If the answer to any of these questions is no, your preparation is incomplete. You have not yet achieved your objective.

Look again at your strategy. Is it sound in light of what you are trying to accomplish? Decide what changes in strat-egy and organization are needed. Modify and adjust until you are convinced that you are using the best method to tell your story. It may be helpful to ask a colleague to listen to the presentation to help evaluate your effectiveness.

Practice

Still, you are not quite done. Your presentation is not complete until you have practiced your talk. There is no magic number of times to rehearse. Some presentations you may have to practice only a few times, others a great deal more. Practice it enough to smooth out the rough spots, to be able to deliver most of it with notes used only as a support, not as a script or crutch. Practice it to the point of confidence in its results.

You can only do this if you practice standing up and speaking out loud. It won't work simply to sit down and think what you might say. If you practice aloud, you'll find that you are able to express the same idea using different words. This will help your presentation sound natural to your audience and will relieve you of the anxiety of trying to remember the exact wording you engineered for that thought.

If you can, rehearse in the same room in which you will be speaking, and have a friend listen to you. This will reduce the anxiety that comes from speaking in an unfamiliar environment and allow you to get more comfortable with being looked at while you talk.

Especially practice the opening, closing, and main points of your talk. Because people tend to judge each other according to instant first impressions, you literally have just a few seconds to initially establish your credibility with the audience. If you don't, it will be hard work to gain it with the rest of your talk, no matter how good it is. Be sure you can open with a strong voice and good eye contact.

Similarly, you must be able to deliver your strongest points with lots of energy and conviction. These are the ideas you want the audience to remember, so pay particular attention to them while practicing. Be sure you can tell your story convincingly.

The audience is going to remember your last words most. Your closing statement, then, should be delivered without notes. To do this, practice the closing without notes until you are comfortable enough with it to give it the right ooomph.

A very important part of rehearsing is timing your presentation. You should always plan to take less time than you've been given. Your audience knows when you're supposed to be finished and will get restless if you don't sound like you're about to close when that time approaches. The only exceptions to this may be if you have a particularly exciting question-and-answer session in progress and your audience has chosen to go overtime. Still, try to close as soon as possible.

Timing is especially critical if you have been given only a few minutes on a tight agenda with other presenters. How many times have you been in a meeting where several people were to give five-minute updates and the first three people took ten minutes each? You probably had a difficult time listening because you just knew you were going to be kept overtime and miss that lunch date you had been looking forward to. Either that, or the only presentation you came to hear was the last one, which will now be dropped from the agenda to stay on schedule. Don't you be the speaker who creates this situation!

Preparing for Mistakes

Although the best way to avoid mistakes is to be thoroughly prepared, all speakers goof once in a while. What do you do if you drop your notes or, worse yet, the glass of water?

What if a slide is projected upside down? Have you ever seen a speaker trip on the microphone cord?

You can be prepared to deal with these situations if you first accept the fact that they will occur. And so what if they do? Just stay calm and roll with it. Don't let mistakes rattle you and make you lose control, and don't say "I'm sorry" or "Excuse me."

If you have your nervousness under control and are letting your natural personality guide you, a mistake can be turned into a very valuable moment of "humanness" between you and your audience. If it's a funny mistake, laugh with them. If not, don't call attention to it other than to pause, smile, and keep right on going.

The best way to prepare for these moments is to imagine all the worst things that could possibly go wrong. Use your visualization skills to envision how you would like to handle that error. Rehearse in your mind casually picking up your notes, reordering them, and starting up again right where you left off. Imagine making a witty remark about the sudden change in weather and stepping away from the spilled water. You'll be surprised how easy it is to overcome those dreaded goofs, and your audience will be so impressed!

Whenever you have a presentation to make, remember the following steps in preparing for effective communication.

- Select a subject.

- Determine a specific, limited objective.

- Plan your strategy.

- Organize your ideas.

- Evaluate what you have written.

- Practice.

Chapter 3

STRATEGY: ANALYZING YOUR AUDIENCE

As discussed in the previous section, the first two steps of preparing for a presentation are selecting your topic and determining your objective. These two are fairly straightforward. Once you have chosen an objective, you may be tempted to jump to organizing. This, however, omits the pivotal step of planning the technique you will use to present your story. You must plan your strategy.

Why a strategy? Because in varying degrees we all have a desire to satisfy our own particular interests and needs. Take the time to learn your listeners' interests; design your presentation to appeal to them and you will greatly improve your chances for success.

Audience Analysis

It is essential that you know exactly who your audience is so that you can tailor your presentation to the specific group of people to whom you will be speaking. Talk with the person who invited you to speak and find out as much of the following as possible.

- Age

- Male, female, or both

- Political and social concerns

- Educational background

- Religion

- Occupation

- Extent of knowledge of the subject

- Feelings toward the subject (pro or con, resistant, sympathetic, etc.)

- Time of day you will speak (right after cocktails or a heavy meal?)

- Mood of the meeting (formal or informal)

- Audience size

- How long you are expected to speak

- What or who precedes and follows you on the agenda

In addition, it's helpful to ask your contact person for the names of a couple of people who will be in the audience. Call them, tell them you are preparing your talk, and ask what they are interested in hearing. Then try to meet these people when you arrive for your presentation. This will give you a few friendly faces in the crowd to help you over those opening jitters.

Audience Interests

The selection of the proper audience interests is complicated by the individuality of people. However, every person in your audience has basic human needs. Your presentation will be much stronger if you appeal to those needs and show how your message can satisfy them. Five basic needs, as described in the book *Open Management* (see Bibliography), are:

- economic well-being

- control over one's life

- recognition

- security

- a sense of belonging

These are deep inner areas of audience interests. The order of importance will vary with each person. When speaking to a group, you won't be able to determine the individual's needs. Therefore, your presentation must demonstrate how all of these needs can be satisfied by accepting your idea. Following are some examples of words and phrases that can be used in your presentation to translate people's basic human needs into areas of interest.

Economic Well-Being
money-saving
wise investment
your money's worth
fits your budget
a secure economic decision

Control Over One's Life
become the leader
the decision is in your hands
have it your way
right at your fingertips
fits your schedule

Recognition
be the first to . . .
highest-ranking
be seen as wise decision maker
stand out in the crowd
VIP treatment

Security
safe
your assurance of
put your mind at ease
you can depend on
always there when you need us

A Sense of Belonging
join the crowd
everyone's doing it this way
widespread acceptance
recommended by more . . .
best-selling

Finding the best audience interests to use in your strategy is like trying to pick a good car: You must take advantage of intuition, emotion, and logic to limit the gamble. Good strategy will improve your chances of selling your story, so the time devoted to searching for the best strategy is well spent.

Recall any personal contact you may have had with the audience. The best strategy is based on personal likes and dislikes, the needs and priorities of the listeners. The majority of your communication will be with people you know, so be prepared for the day when you will need to know their interests. As you meet and work with people, practice listening well. Try to recognize and learn their needs and interests.

The background or common interests of your audience will yield some suggestions. Before speaking to the American Institute of Electrical and Electronic Engineers, for example, you could check the membership requirements to find that the majority are college graduates who work in the electrical engineering field. These two facts alone would give you some good ideas on an approach to this audience.

There is always some clue present that will help you bracket your listeners' interests and show your story in the best light. Take the time to find it!

Using Audience Interests to Strategize

When you have selected the best audience interests, use them in a strategy to gain and keep the attention of your listeners.

Strategy helps arouse initial audience attention. The opening of a presentation is always difficult. Without a feel for the interests of your audience, it can be impossible. If your audience was a group of chefs and you said, "The microchip is the symbol of your profession," you would most likely be met with a sea of baffled looks. That statement might be all right for computer scientists, but not for chefs. For this group, a more appropriate opening might be, "The menu is the symbol of your profession."

Strategy helps you state your objective in the language of the listener. You could help a construction foreman to be more careful in preparing vouchers by stating that in doing so he would "speed up the preparation of the company profit-and-loss statement." While this may be true, you may get a better response if you said, "You can help us improve the records for keeping your paycheck right."

Strategy helps you prove your points. The examples you choose will be most effective if they are in tune with the interests of your audience. Using examples of successful college graduates to instill confidence and ambition in apprentice course trainees is obviously the wrong selection. But to tell them of apprentice graduates who have progressed to section and general-manager status is a truthful example that may appeal to their point of view.

Strategy also helps in reaching a successful conclusion. You must know the capabilities of your audience members before you ask them to take a specific action: You don't ask a plumber to fix your television set. Even when you ask a person to do something she is capable of, do it diplomatically: "Ruth, all we need to finish the appropriation for your new project is a report on the hours of the consultant's time involved. Would you please get it to me by noon tomorrow?''

The "You" Attitude

You can say anything better when you have the interests of your audience in mind. One very good approach that can help you think in terms of your audience's point of view is to use the word *you* as you prepare your presentation. Think carefully of every instance where you want to use *I* or *we*. Try to rephrase the sentence or thought so that you will be using the word *you* instead. This will automatically help you think in terms of audience interests, and will help you sound as if you are considering them.

Of course, you will continue to use *I* and *we* in your talks. When you refer to your own actions and opinions, you can't avoid the use of *I*. Similarly, *us* may be effective when your reference is mildly chiding or derogatory such as, ''All of us can stand improvement.''

You might use *we* when you are calling for a unified action by you and everyone in the audience. But be certain you want unified action before you use it. ''We must all move as a body from this auditorium and protest this action tonight.'' ''We should go up and see Collins right now.'' These are examples of unified action.

Use *you* if you want individual action. ''You should fill out one of these forms before you leave tonight.'' ''You ought to take this up to Collins right now.''

The use of the word *you* won't solve all the problems of appealing to audience interests, but it will help you think in the right direction. Try it in your next presentation.

Being Genuine

While audience interest is the true core of a good strategy,
you must go further than just planning the words. You have
to carry sincere concern for your listeners into your presentation. A "phony" approach, one which doesn't really appeal
to your audience, can destroy the entire story. Plan a genuine
strategy and then use your voice, gestures, everything about
you to prove your sincerity.

Think about your speaking style as you look at the following lists of things that audiences like or dislike in a speaker or
presentation.

Likes	Dislikes
Friendliness	Sarcasm
Cheerfulness	Facetiousness
Believability	Arrogance
Emphasizing the positive	Anticlimaxes
Mystery or suspense (which is solved)	Talkativeness
Keeping things moving toward the objective	Obstinacy
	Ridicule
Humor	Contradiction
Variety	Smugness
Enthusiasm	Criticism
Storytelling	Dishonesty
Sincerity	Lecturing or preaching
Logic	Condescension
Modesty	

Once you have prepared a talk based on your analysis of
the audience, keep in mind that if you are making that same
presentation to another audience, you'll need to reevaluate
your strategy. You won't have to plan from scratch, but you'll

have to shift your approach to match the audience every time you give that presentation. Learn to be audience-specific.

There is a right way and a wrong way to tell every story. The right way to tell yours is to use a strategy based on the interests of your audience. You might think there are special instances where this does not apply. But look at it this way: You should always look for some way to approach your talk from the audience's point of view.

If you have great difficulty in finding a sincere interest on which to establish your strategy, consider seriously whether you should be telling your story at all. No presentation is better than the appeal it has for the audience. If there is no appeal, there is no reason to tell the story. The interests of your audience are uppermost in their minds. If you want to be heard, make sure their interests are uppermost in *your* mind.

Chapter 4

ORGANIZING YOUR PRESENTATION

There are literally dozens of approaches to organizing your presentation. Each is designed to help you open strong, stay on target, and close with a summary or call to action.

The following formula will give you a systematic way to approach preparing for a presentation. It's easy to use, is an excellent example of the kind of strategy we have been discussing, and is adaptable to most occasions, subjects, and audiences.

The formula works so well because it is based on the reactions of the listener. It anticipates the listener's mental inertia and objections, and gives you the means to overcome them. The formula has five points:

- Get Attention
- Give Main Points
- Give Examples
- Give Benefits
- Get Results

Suppose you have just stepped out on the platform or stood up in a staff meeting. Facing you is a roomful of faces—your audience. What are they thinking? It might be that some of them are really eager to hear what you have to say. But it is safer to assume that—as they lean back and drift into silence—

they are all thinking about unmade phone calls, unanswered letters, incomplete reports, or lists of errands to do. Your job is to:

Get Attention

Before you begin, assume that your audience is completely apathetic. They may be, in fact, muttering to themselves, "I wonder if this is going to be any good." Plan to overcome that apathy by using a strong opening, one that will immediately catch their attention and give them a reason to listen to you.

The first words out of your mouth should not be boring ones, such as, "Today I'm going to talk about . . ." Let's take the example of a staff meeting. Suppose one of the managers is going to summarize the results of a task-force study. She begins, "I would like to take the next hour or so to describe the detailed deliberations of the study we have just concluded, delving into certain economies and efficiencies that might be achieved to . . ."

Gee, I wish I had gone to the gym instead. . . .

Suppose that manager began by saying, "Just nine weeks ago today the task force met to find out what was wrong with this operation, what made it one of the most expensive in the company. You may find what we've discovered about ourselves hard to believe. . . ."

The narrative flavor and the hint of something important to come gets their interest and arouses their curiosity fast.

Curiosity and interest can be captured equally well with a direct challenge, a well-told anecdote, a paraphrased quotation or saying, or by a question. If a question, it might be one to which you really want an answer, or a rhetorical question, but when you use a rhetorical question, always be ready for the joker in the audience who will answer it loudly and throw you off-track.

All attention-getting openings are designed to combat the apathetic attitude of your audience and focus their thinking on your topic. Don't open with an irrelevant "warm-up" story or joke you heard last week. This looks to your audience like you are nervous and afraid to begin your talk. Instead, be sure that your opening statement and actions are related to the message you want to communicate and are not "gimmicky" or overdone.

Assume that you have gained your audience's attention. You also must tell them what's in it for them to listen to you. You need to offer some suggestions of how your presentation will have some positive impact on them. So, after you've gotten their attention, you need to:

Give Main Points

This is the body of your presentation. To be effective it is essential that you focus on your objective and the method that will best achieve it. Your purpose may be to:

- inform

- persuade

- sell

- create interest

- inspire

- ask for a decision, or

- initiate action

Whatever your purpose, you need to develop your main points based on your audience analysis. What do they need to hear? What can be left out? Your job is to sift through all your information and come up with a concise, interesting way to present your message.

Don't try to include too many points or your material will become unclear. Each point you present should be critical to your audience's understanding of your message. If it isn't, leave it out. To support your main points:

Give Examples

This step requires that you support your main points with specific examples. Related and appropriate anecdotes make for highly interesting and convincing material. Statistics, quotations, and analogies will help remove doubt from your listener's mind.

Illustrate your points with as many stories about people as you can; your audience will appreciate this personal touch and respond to it positively. The format of a well-constructed point includes:

- general statement of the point or idea

- proof given in the form of anecdotes, examples, statistics, etc.

- restatement of the point.

By keeping these aspects in mind, each point you want to make is a separate unit by itself—a neat, convincing, self-sufficient package. Limit the number of points you explore to the number you can adequately prove within the limitations imposed.

So far so good. Your audience has been aroused from its apathetic attitude. They understand your objective. They are convinced of your main points by your use of interesting examples. Now they are ready for you to:

Give Benefits

Tell your listeners what benefits they can gain by accepting your idea, buying your product, or taking action. Whatever the purpose of your presentation, you must answer the basic human question of "What's in it for me?" by letting them know how the subject affects them personally. Your answer to this question should:

- logically follow the examples you have used.

- reflect your presentation objective.

- demonstrate why the audience should be interested and/or how they will benefit from the action you want them to take or the information you want them to absorb.

If you have been clear about the benefits to the listener, it is time to:

Get Results

What are you expecting your audience to do as a result of your speech? Your presentation has a purpose, and this is the time to sum it up and ask for action. The salesperson asks the customer to buy, the politician asks for votes, the lawyer asks for a verdict, and the staff-meeting presenter says, "So much for the highlights of our findings. As you leave, *pick* up a copy of the detailed report. *Read* it carefully in the next week and *make note* of any ideas you have. We will meet on the fourteenth to *lay plans* for improvement. See you then."

In any presentation, the conclusion should be as strong and forceful as you can legitimately make it. It always derives from your presentation objective. If your objective was to persuade the audience to take some action, ask for it in your final statements. But be sure that whatever you ask for is appropriate and within the audience's power to achieve.

A talk to explain or inform, however, may not have a strong bid for action. In this case, you need to tell the audience how you want them to apply the information, or what's in it for them to know this information. You may also wish to tell them how to find out more on the subject you've covered. Just make certain your closing is in tune with your objective, and you will be doing the right thing.

One trap many speakers fall into is the "disclaimer" at the end of a speech. Avoid the tendency to say, "I hope that demonstrates the importance of . . ." or "I think that outlines . . ." Your closing should be a strong, definite statement. "That demonstrates the importance of . . ." or "That outlines . . ."

Remember, you know you have accomplished your objective because of your thorough planning and practicing. You will only get the results you want if you demonstrate this confidence to your audience in a dynamite closing.

Those are the five steps on which to base the organization of your ideas. Each step builds upon the previous one, and all lead to a strong conclusion. The five-step formula will build audience interest as you progress toward your "results." End your presentation at this peak of audience interest, and your listeners will remember your message.

Chapter 5

GETTING IT ON PAPER

Now that you have a system for organizing your presentation, how do you brainstorm for the content? You first need to give yourself some time to sit and think about nothing else. Even just a few minutes of concentrated, uninterrupted time will help you sift through your mental files and come up with the ideas you want.

Once you've done this, you then need to commit these ideas to paper so you can begin to organize them in an orderly fashion. There are a few different ways you can go about doing this. Two are described in the following sections.

Idea Mapping

Idea mapping is a fun way to let your brain go free and get all your ideas down without worrying about whether or not they are good ones, where you will use them, or how you will support them.

Get a large sheet of paper, a good supply of Scotch 3M Post-It® notepads (be sure you choose a size large enough to write key phrases on), and a pen with bright ink. (Pencil will do, but when you're through idea mapping, you aren't going to want to work hard at seeing what you've jotted down. You'll see why in a moment!)

The first step is to write your topic on the top of the sheet in letters large enough to serve as a visual reminder and to keep your thoughts going in that direction. Next, write your objective in the middle of the page. The wording should be brief enough to remind you only of the main idea—don't waste space with a long statement.

Now the fun begins. Simply jot down anything you think of that's related to your topic and objective. Try to use only key words or phrases; this isn't the time to elaborate. Write each idea on one Post-It® and stick it onto the sheet of paper. Anywhere—it doesn't matter now. Your goal is to get all those scattered ideas into one place. Don't throw out any ideas, even if you think they are way out in left field.

If you are speaking in an area of your expertise, you will probably have a tough time writing as fast as your ability to think. If you are trying to tackle what for you is a fairly new topic, this process might be more of a struggle. That's okay— sit down with your reference material while you do this if it will help.

When you begin to feel like a popcorn machine valiantly trying to pop every last kernel, it's time to stop. Take a look at what you have done and start categorizing all your ideas into the different steps of the organizational formula discussed in Chapter 4, Organizing Your Presentation. To do this, start moving your ideas into five areas on the sheet. If it helps, label each area with one of the five steps of the formula: Attention, Main Points, Examples, Benefits, and Results.

Ask yourself which of these ideas jumps out at you as a good attention-getter. Which are benefits to your listeners? Are there some ideas that would work especially well as supporting examples? Maybe you have already written down that dynamite closing without even knowing it.

The beauty of the Post-It® notes is that you can change your mind. Something you had put in the Attention area, you can shift to the Example group.

After you work with your idea map for a while, you will

begin to get a sense of how you want your ideas to be put together. You might find that you have to do a little more research in one area or some additional brainstorming in another, but now you will know what you are looking for.

There are additional steps you'll need to take to get your presentation on paper, but first let's look at a second method of brainstorming.

Idea Card Sorting

This process is essentially the same as idea mapping but uses a different medium. Instead of a large sheet of paper and Post-Its®, you will need a stack of three-by-five index cards. Write your topic on one card and set it down in front of you. Do the same with your objective. This will give you a visual reminder of what you are trying to accomplish.

Now let your mind go, and write down all your ideas on the cards, one idea per card. (As a note; position the cards vertically and write your ideas from top to bottom. You'll find out why as you read on.) When you are through, and ready to organize them, write one step of the formula on each of five cards. Set these in a row on your desk as though you were setting up to play solitaire. Now sort through your idea cards, placing each one below the formula step you think it most fits. Again, you can go back and change your mind about any of them.

In this way you can "rewrite" your presentation many times simply by rearranging your cards. Add cards for new ideas and throw out irrelevant ones until you have a rough framework for your talk.

Creating Notes

Some people feel the need to write out their entire presentation word for word. This can be dangerous, because you can get caught in the trap of sounding too canned and mechanical. Trying to express each idea exactly the way you wrote it tends to make you lose your natural expressiveness and reduces the impact of your message.

If it helps you to write the whole thing out to get an idea of how it will sound, okay. But don't use a script to present the talk. Instead, work from your script in developing an outline to use in the actual presentation. (Also, see Chapter 10, Types of Speeches, for hints on how to read a speech effectively.) The following suggestions will help you develop your own outlines.

Use your idea map or cards to arrive at a rough sketch of what you will say. Then, before you go any further, stand up and start talking. Of course, it won't be the polished presentation you want, but it will help you think in terms of conversational words, not written words, and will help you get an idea of how it will flow. You might want to do some rearranging at this point, then try talking it through again. Do this until you have a fair idea of what you're going to say. Try expressing each idea in more than one way, using different words to avoid sounding as if you memorized it.

Now create your outline. All you need is a guideline to keep you on track and remind you of key points. Note any statistics or names you want to use correctly, and jot down any phrases that need to be said in a certain way to be effective.

Then practice your talk a few more times both with and without your notes, striving for the most natural delivery you can achieve. You will be surprised how firmly in mind your presentation is planted.

Be sure you get to this "comfort level" with your presentation about twenty-four hours before the time you will deliver it. This "cushion" gives you a chance to get the rest you need without worrying about what you will say, and it gives your talk a chance to "marinate" and achieve the right flavor.

Samples of note outlines appear below. Note that on the three-by-five card you write vertically. This is because it fits in your hand more comfortably, is easier to read, and is less distracting. The amount of information you put on each card will vary depending on how large you need the words to be so you can read them. You might also leave space for other reminders, such as, "Flip chart" or "Distribute samples." Be sure to number your cards, and only write on one side.

**Three-by-five
Card Outline***

> I. What fear most?
>   A. Heights, fire, death?
>   B. Most often named—
>   public speaking
>
> II. Human nature what it is . . .
>   A. We don't do something
>   terrified of
>   B. Why stand up and try to
>   make sense?
>
> III. Reasons:
>   A. Careers
>   1. Face-to-face
>   2. Seen as professional,
>   competent
>   a. (Personal
>   experience)

*This is an example of an *outline* to be used as a cue card while speaking and should not be confused with an idea card. Smaller than actual size.

Full-Page Outline

Relax
Get Set
Eye Contact
Smile   What fear most?
                Heights, fire, death?
                Most often named—speaking

         Human nature what it is . . . (Main Points)
                We don't do something we're terrified of
         Why stand up/try to make sense?

         Reasons:
         Careers
Eye Contact   Face-to-face
            Seen as professional
            (personal experience)

         Personal Life
            Buying car
            Boring dinner

Make it fun! More important:
            Changes perception of self

Giving It a Title

Sometimes you won't need to worry about a title for your presentation. But often you will be asked for it, either for the person introducing you or for a printed agenda.

The title is an important part of your presentation: How many times have you decided whether or not to read a book, see a movie, or listen to a speaker based on the title alone? The fact is, people will have an impression of you and your presentation from even those few words. Since this is the case, why not use words that will pique their curiosity? It's a little like the attention-getter discussed earlier; the title should stimulate your audience's interest in the topic.

How do you pick a good title? Titles that explain what your speech is about are sometimes acceptable. But it would be much better to think of an exciting way to entice people to want to listen to you. Here are a few examples:

Acceptable: The Budget System for the Next Quarter
Better: Budget—How Much Can I Spend in the Next Quarter?

Acceptable: How to Motivate People
Better: Getting a Kick Out of Work

Acceptable: The Future of Our Business
Better: Our Business—A Look Into the Crystal Ball

Acceptable: Why You Need to Improve Communication Skills
Better: Effective Communication—Who Needs It?

Try to be creative with your titles. What you call your presentation can have a great effect on the mood of the audience when they come to listen to you. So be aware of the atmosphere your title creates. Keep your title simple, straightforward, and, if appropriate, fun.

Chapter 6

YOUR SPEAKING STRENGTHS

An important aspect of being an effective communicator is knowing and utilizing your own personal strengths. There are many "rules" about speaking: the only real rule is do what you do best. This is what makes the difference between a speech maker and an effective communicator.

Identifying Your Strengths

How can you know what you do well? We spend so much time trying to work on what we see as weaknesses that we forget all about what we excel in. This is also true in speaking. You may have a dynamic voice or excellent eye contact and not even know it because you are so concerned about your lack of gestures. Your concern becomes so overwhelming that you let it diminish your voice, and your lack of confidence can destroy your eye contact. In this way, focusing too much attention on your weaknesses undermines your strengths.

If, on the other hand, you focus on and believe in your dynamic voice and excellent eye contact, you will feel more confident and comfortable. Achieving greater comfort is the key that will allow you to add a few more gestures—naturally—each time you speak. And the key to achieving that ease is finding out what you do well in the first place.

Discovering your strengths can be done on your own, but a "buddy system" is usually more effective. This is because people really have a hard time complimenting themselves and really believing it. Hearing a compliment from someone else somehow makes it more real. Videotape can be extremely useful, but working with a friend (who knows something about communication!) can also be powerful.

First, prepare a short presentation. Three to five minutes is all you need. Deliver the presentation all the way through, without interruption. If you lose your train of thought or say something you don't like, fine. Keep on going to the end. If you have videotaped the presentation, when you view the tape, your job is to pinpoint several strengths you already have in place. You will find it helpful to use the following checklist to help identify the strengths you exhibit. At this time don't worry about areas for improvement; that comes later. So, no negatives here, and don't be so nit-picking! Concentrate on seeing what you do well.

If you are not using videotape, you will need someone to take notes while you speak, jotting down those things you did well. You may even go through the presentation a second time, allowing yourself to be stopped when you demonstrate a strength so you can think about what you just did. Here are some strength areas you will be looking for.

Check those areas in which the speaker demonstrates skill.

PREPARATION

Opening
A strong, well-prepared beginning, powerful
enough to attract audience attention.   _____

Strategy
The way the material is presented is relevant
to the audience.   _____

Closing
A strong summary of key points and a clear
"results" statement. _____

Compliance with Time
Completes the presentation in the time allotted. _____

CREDIBILITY

Eye Contact/Connection
Uses eye contact to make this a two-way
communication. _____

Delivery
Full inflection, natural word rate, pauses. Conversational. _____

Intensity
Demonstrates sincerity, enthusiasm, conviction. Appropriate vocal variety and volume. _____

DEMEANOR

Presence
Appropriate dress, appearance, and groom-
ing. Sets up and controls the physical surroundings to enhance the presentation. _____

Stance/Gestures
Confident stance, smooth walking (if called
for); gestures in a natural way to support the
verbal message. _____

Notes/Visuals
Notes are unobtrusive. Visuals are well-
prepared and managed professionally. _____

CONTENT

Analysis
Approach to the subject is original, interesting. Central idea or objective is clear. Selects
appropriate listener benefits. _____

Material
   Provides sufficient facts, examples, and illustrations to support main points.   _____

Organization
   Includes introduction, body, and conclusion. Good development of ideas; logical flow.   _____

Building on Your Strengths

Now that you have identified your strengths, it's important to concentrate on using and capitalizing on them. A few good strengths, well utilized, make for a more effective communicator than someone who is continually focusing on improving their weaknesses. The "80/20 rule" applies here: You should spend 80% of your time building on your strengths and only 20% of your time on areas for improvement. In this way you establish a strong foundation. This allows you to be yourself and excel in communicating a sincere message rather than focusing on technical perfection.

Applying Your Strengths

Knowing your strengths is not only an important part of gaining confidence and presenting yourself well, but also is an important ingredient in matching your special blend of talents to the best speaking situations for you.

   Speaking successfully depends on a combination of your style and your content and the setting. Following is a list of questions you should ask yourself as you evaluate your effectiveness in a variety of situations.

• Is the content within my area of strength?

• Do I enjoy talking about it?

- Am I comfortable with the audience size?

- Which of my style strengths can I utilize in this situation?

- Is the level of formality or informality consistent with my strengths?

- Can I state my message adequately in the time given?

- Am I comfortable with the setup of the room?

- Am I comfortable with the audience's expectations of me?

There may be additional questions you need to ask yourself to be certain you are walking into a situation that allows you to capitalize on your strengths. As you can see, this relies on a good understanding of what you do well, and on a good audience analysis.

So that you can build on your successes, beginning speakers may want to speak only in settings that allow them to do their best. As you gain confidence, stretch yourself by trying more difficult situations.

The next chapter will give you some specific techniques for using your strengths to build confidence.

Chapter 7

VISUALIZATION

One of the most important influences on your ability to speak
and communicate well is your perception of yourself. All too
often there is more emphasis placed on the negative rather
than the positive. Over a period of time this creates a lower
self-image than if your positive traits and successes were
complimented. The result is a lack of confidence when con-
fronting certain situations. A well-proven method of overcoming this negative self-perception is visualization.

What Is It?

The dictionary defines *visualization* as "the forming of mental visual images." It is the ability to picture yourself in a
specific situation and visualize what happens and what you
do. In any given situation, you have a *choice* as to whether
you apply negative visualization or positive visualization:
Will you see yourself as failing or succeeding? It's up to you.

The act of visualization will have tremendous impact on
the results of the real situation. Therefore, positive visualization can set you up to succeed. Unfortunately, most people
are better at negative visualization since this is often what
they have learned over a lifetime. Years of negative visualization result in negative "tapes" that we play over and over in
our minds, that convince us that we will not be able to
accomplish a certain task. Positive visualization means learn-

ing to remake these tapes, replacing them with positive images of ourselves succeeding.

Positive visualization is what sports psychology is all about, and it is this visualization that is commonly used by athletes to help prepare them to perform at their best. A good example of its effectiveness in sports is an experiment involving a basketball team. The coach divided the team into two groups to see which could most improve its free-throw shooting. One group practiced shooting every day, while the other group practiced only in their mind's eye, seeing themselves make every shot. When the two groups competed, those who visualized making all the shots outscored their teammates.

By consciously visualizing yourself doing an activity positively, you give your body the opportunity to respond successfully, whether it is shooting free throws or speaking. Your level of confidence when you face a speaking situation depends on how well you have prepared yourself both externally and internally—your material and your mind. Using positive visualization to influence your performance is an important part of your overall preparation. If you play negative tapes as you practice or deliver your presentation, you will not be as successful as if you play positive tapes, just as the athlete who doesn't focus on potential mistakes but on top performance.

Applying Visualization

The process of visualization appears to be simple, and in some ways it is. The difficult part is the self-discipline necessary to concentrate and make it real for you. Following is how you can use visualization to prepare for a successful delivery.

Step 1—Focus on your strengths. In your mind's eye, see yourself in a specific speaking situation. Concentrate. Observe yourself performing in a way that uses your speaking strengths. This will help you believe in your ability to succeed and build your confidence. You might ask a friend to watch you deliver a presentation and help you identify what you do well, or use videotape to help you do this for yourself. (Chapter 6 will help you with this step.)

Step 2—Select a specific speaking skill that you would like to improve. You might choose smoother gestures, controlling nervousness, or handling your visuals better. At first, it is important to select only one specific skill at a time. Again, a friend or videotape can be helpful. Choose the one skill you think will make the most difference in your next presentation.

Step 3—Create a visual image of yourself performing this skill well. Again, imagine yourself in a specific situation. See yourself using your strengths and correctly doing the one thing you want to change. It may help to observe a few speakers who demonstrate the effective presentation skills described in this book. There are a few good videotapes available that provide models of good speaking skills. Remember, however, that you are you, and you should have your own style.

Step 4—Focus on this positive visual image often. To create positive tapes, focus on these positive images of yourself performing successfully. This is when self-discipline and concentration are critical. You need to plan time for your visualization exercises in addition to all your other preparation and practice. As you rewrite and practice portions of your presentation, you must also take time to visualize the changes in how you will look and sound. And, of course, be sure to do your visualization the night before your presentation.

This is the process of creating positive tapes. By mentally visualizing yourself as a success in any speaking situation, your chances of achieving this are greatly increased. Whether you are concerned about thinking on your feet, projecting your voice, or answering difficult questions, this works. The more often you practice positive visualization, the clearer the picture will become. You will be giving yourself a powerful source of confidence in your ability to communicate well. If you've done your visualization homework, once you're in the presentation you can relax and just let it flow.

One of the tricks to letting visualization work for you is to have a very clear picture of the environment in which you will be speaking. Ask lots of questions so that you will know how large your audience is, how they will be dressed, how the room is set up, and what its probable ambience will be. It is also helpful to review the audience analysis you conducted as part of your preparation so that you can focus on who the audience is. Then, as you practice your visualization, you can place yourself in that environment. If you have a chance to visit the actual room ahead of time, you'll be able to visualize the setting even more accurately. Try to arrange at least one practice in the room if you can.

Practice Exercises

Here are some exercises you can use to get started. Once you get the hang of it, you will be able to develop your own visualization exercises to mentally prepare for a variety of speaking situations. Each of the following exercises will give you a few specific steps to visualize. Take yourself through each exercise several times to get a feel for letting your mind's eye create the image you want to project.

EXERCISE 1: THE ENVIRONMENT

• What are you wearing?

• What does the room look like?

- Where will you be sitting/standing?

- Who is the audience?

- What does the audience look like?

- What audiovisual equipment is present?

- Where is the equipment positioned?

Spend a few moments simply visualizing this environment. Get comfortable with the surroundings. The advantage of doing this is that when you deliver your presentation, you will feel as though you have been there before. You will not feel as strange in the room as you might otherwise, and this greatly adds to your effectiveness.

EXERCISE 2: THE OPENING

- You are being introduced; listen carefully.

- Get up out of your chair.

- Stand up straight.

- Breathe deeply as you walk.

- Walk calmly and confidently.

- Smile at the audience.

- Pause and gain your stance, place your notes or outline in an unobtrusive but easily accessible place.

- Greet your audience with your eyes.

- Start your opening lines with a clear, strong voice.

This will help you deal with the extra nervousness you feel at the beginning of a presentation. Since you have only a few seconds to establish your credibility, visualizing the opening will help you do your very best to deliver your first sentences effectively, connect with the audience, and gain their attention immediately.

EXERCISE 3: VISUALS

(This visualization exercise should be done after you have selected and designed the visual(s) you will use.)

- Imagine where and how your visual is set up.

- Where are you standing in relation to it?

- Introduce/reveal the visual.

- Allow the audience time to absorb the visual.

- Comment on the visual as needed.

- Put away the visual or move to the next one smoothly.

The important element in this exercise is to spend adequate time visualizing the mechanics of your visual. Whether you will be handling paper or pushing buttons, visualize yourself doing so professionally. This means you have to spend time learning how to use it, and practicing it for real as well! Then you can put your visualization to work for you.

EXERCISE 4: QUESTIONS

- Summarize your main points.

- Pause.

- Invite questions.

- Pause, listen, smile.

- Hear yourself being asked a question.

- Look at the questioner while you listen.

- Pause.

- Answer briefly, looking at everyone.

- Go on to the next question.

As part of your preparation for your presentation and for this exercise, you will need to think about, and perhaps formulate, some of the questions you are likely to be asked. If you think you will get hostile questions, refer to some of the suggestions in Chapter 13. Visualize yourself calmly handling the toughest situation you can think of, and you will do well when it actually happens.

As you can see, a visualization exercise is easy to develop and use. In the beginning, tackle one small piece of a presentation at a time. Slowly build toward the image you want to project. Remember to capitalize on your strengths and consistently work on improving skills one by one.

Chapter 8

DELIVERING A STRONG MESSAGE

After listening to a speech, a discerning listener said, "He didn't have much to say, but he did a nice job of saying it." This is perhaps the most cutting criticism that can be leveled at a speaker. It means, very simply, that the speaker merely wasted the listener's time—albeit in a somewhat entertaining fashion.

Every good presentation must "have something to say." It must be built upon your desire to deliver a meaningful message to the audience; to communicate new information, new ideas, or a new approach to a familiar subject. The presentation must reward the listener for the time invested in listening to it, and the speaker for the time invested in preparing it. But the presentation can provide these rewards only if it is factually full and convincing.

Your "having something to say" depends upon your willingness to gather facts relevant to your topic, your ability to present those facts in an original and imaginative way, and your ability to persuade your audience to embrace your objective.

Facts That Will Convince

The most vital element in convincing any listener that your objective and your message are worthwhile is your ability to prove your statements. There are several good tools to use in doing this.

- **Statistics.** Use figures in their proper context, but don't use too many, and be sure to round off the numbers.

- **Example.** State merely that something has happened; or describe a situation, story, or anecdote in support of your point.

- **Illustration.** Give a more detailed statement of the situation or event.

- **Authority.** Quote or refer to someone the audience knows and respects.

- **Analogy.** Compare the unknown to the nearest known.

- **Explanation.** "Show and tell" your listeners how a point works so they'll know why it's better.

- **Restatement.** If your point is important enough, repeat it in different terms.

Each of these tools can be valuable in helping you make a convincing presentation, but select them carefully. Some subjects demand more emphasis on the emotions, so you'll want to use a number of personal, or people-oriented, stories. Other subjects may require a battery of statistics or authority "endorsements." Generally, an effective presentation is a blend of several of these tools. The resulting mix will have emotional impact, logic, and authority—and therefore the power to convince.

Even before you begin thinking about the organization of your next presentation, ask yourself, "Is there enough solid material here to convince me that my point is valid?" If the answer is less than "Absolutely," you have more digging to do before you begin organizing the presentation.

Expressing Ideas Concisely

"Brevity," says one authority, "means rather extreme economy in the use of words, as in a telegram. Conciseness means brevity plus completeness. That is, the idea of conciseness is carried out properly if a speech is as short as possible and at the same time includes everything necessary." Following are some useful hints to improve conciseness.

- Omit meaningless, unnecessary introductions.

- Avoid run-on sentences. Your thoughts will be more clearly expressed by using sentences with definite beginnings and endings. Pausing will help you with this.

- Use short sentences in preference to long ones, but a good balance of both. Be sure each sentence is clear, regardless of its length.

- Avoid redundancy. Shakespeare wrote: "An honest tale speeds best when plainly told."

- Study what you have written to see how many words could be left out without omitting anything essential.

- Although repetition is a good teaching tool, be careful not to repeat in the same way what you have already said. Rather, put a "new frame on an old picture."

- State the central idea first, then elaborate only as necessary.

Expressing Ideas Forcefully

Whatever your natural speaking style, you need to express yourself with strength and conviction. Some people, however, naturally have more forceful personalities than others.

Here are a few questions you can ask yourself to determine your own forcefulness.

- Do you have positive convictions, or are you neutral in most matters?

- Do you try to talk in an entertaining manner?

- Do people look interested when you talk, or do they appear bored and restless?

- Do friends ask you for advice, or do they avoid discussing their concerns with you?

- Do you carry your share of the conversational load, or do you sit back and let others do the talking?

- Finally, do you try for variety in your conversation, or do you have a small vocabulary that you work to the limit?

While these questions relate to how you may interact with people, they will also help you to be aware of ways in which you can develop a more energetic personality. Following are some specific techniques you can use to develop forcefulness in your presentation style.

- Use strong openings and closings in your sentences, your paragraphs, and the entire presentation.

- Use positive, not negative, words.

- Avoid using *I*. Get the *you* attitude.

- Use powerful and descriptive phrases.

- Use action verbs.

- Be imaginative.

- Make your presentation clear and concise.

Originality and Imagination

The secret of being an interesting speaker is simply this: Use your imagination to paint vivid word-pictures that will capture the imagination of your audience. The use of power phrases and action verbs are strong, dynamic tools to arouse imagination.

For example, did you ever hear anyone say, "He hasn't much spine?" Since that description has been overused, it's lost any vivid impact it may once have had. Let's take the same idea and, with a few simple words, put it this way: "There's a dessert named after him—Jell-O!" Does that flash a more vivid picture of a personality?

There is great power in little words. One classic illustration of this occurred during World War II after bombers had roared over England night and day, week after week. Churchill rose in the House of Commons to pay tribute to the gallant but vastly outnumbered Royal Air Force. Picture the time, the place, the occasion. Words seemed futile. Churchill uttered these simple words: "Never in the history of human conflict have so many owed so much to so few." Sixteen small words, yet there's a power in them that stirred minds and gripped hearts.

As a speaker, you must transfer an idea or thought from your mind to your listener's. By limbering up your own imagination, you can become skillful enough to induce your audience to envision the picture you want in just a few words. The use of similarities or contrasts already familiar to the listener, but combined with imagination, are two of the most successful methods for producing lively interest. Notice the striking picture created in your mind by the use of a single phrase showing similarity: "As silent as breeze-scattered dandelion seeds." Or note the use of contrasts, combined in an original manner: "A remark as pointless as a circle."

If you attempt to fill in every detail of your picture, as a competent draftsperson would do for a construction job, you'll inevitably lose the interest of your audience. They don't have the time—or patience—to wait while you plow through a mass of unnecessary detail. Be sure that you give them enough, but not too much, enabling them to create in their minds, accurately and clearly, the word-picture you are presenting.

Imagination can be developed like a muscle and you can learn how to get ideas just as you learn to swim. Learn to retain in your memory thought-provoking word combinations, then incorporate them into your presentations to arouse your listener's interest and imagination. Aren't the following effectively vivid?

- She stuck as close to him as lint on a navy-blue suit.

- As informal as a puppy.

- She gave me a look that would have raised the dead.

Proper use of suspense is also helpful in arousing imagination and maintaining interest. It is widely used in advertising as a means of capturing attention. But remember, people like to have the mystery solved! So don't leave them hanging.

Variety

To be interesting, the word-pictures that you are trying to create must have life and movement. This is accomplished by changing the pattern of your speaking. Sameness is dull, drab, and boring. For example, if all your sentences are about the same length and in the same word order, they become as monotonous as a ticking clock.

Life itself is interesting because it is constantly changing. Good speaking must also contain change—the essence of variety and spiciness. Notice the refreshing variety in the following descriptive phrases.

- Her life is an open book—and she likes to read from it.

- My heart was going like a woodpecker.

- When you ask him what time it is, he wants to tell you how the watch is made.

- His manner is that of a blacksmith with an anvil.

Give your word-pictures variety. Revise your presentations until you have injected them with life and color. Remember, though the phrase itself has become cliché, variety really is the spice of life! Here are some hints that can add color and impact to your next presentation.

- **Keep it specific.** If you're trying to prove that a proposed bond issue is worth less than it will cost, don't tell your listeners that it will "cost the city's taxpayers a huge sum of money." Instead, tell the listener, "It will cost you $85 out of your own pocket and give you a $65 piece of school."

- **Keep it familiar.** Use terms and words you are reasonably sure your listeners will understand. This is an especially important consideration for the specialist addressing a general audience. In such a situation, good word-pictures may be essential.

- **Keep it original.** Don't say the same thing, in the same way, that someone else has. You've heard listeners say, "Not that old story again!" Your word-picture should have both life and movement. For example: "Study this proposal. And I don't mean just stick your big toe in—take a belly flop!"

Next time you are preparing a presentation, think about facts, imagination, and originality. Accumulate all the facts you can, and then put your imagination to work in selecting, arranging, and breathing life into that body of fact. You can then be confident that you will "have something to say" and will reward your listeners—and yourself—for the time invested in that presentation.

Principles of Persuasion

You use it every day. And the deftness with which you use it can mean the difference between having and not having many of the things you want in life. "It" is persuasion—the act of causing a person to believe or do something. Persuasion is known by many names, depending upon the circumstances under which it is used. It has been called influencing, coaxing, convincing, assuring, advertising, inducing, winning over, motivating, converting, selling—to name only a few of its tags.

When we think of selling, we usually visualize a salesperson extolling the virtues of a product. But when we change the word *product* to *idea,* we begin to realize that as speakers we are, in fact, salespeople too.

Selling may be defined as the process of transmitting a desire for action or understanding from yourself to another person. The definition of selling and persuasion are, therefore, the same. Persuasion is selling, and selling is only accomplished by the use of persuasion. In this sense, all of us are salespeople. We must sell our goods, services, ideas, enthusiasm, ourselves. All day long you are actually engaged in being a good salesperson. How can you use this skill with a reasonable assurance of success?

Often our methods of persuasion are applied in a haphazard, almost unconscious way. Analyzing the psychology behind persuasion and becoming more acutely aware of the techniques will result in its controlled, planned use.

The process of persuasion is apparent in both everyday conversations and in more formal presentations where the free exchange of remarks is at least to some degree limited. Whether you are explaining to your spouse the advantages of a mountain vacation or presenting your opinions on how to improve a service, you should know and apply the principles of persuasion if you want to succeed.

Persuasion is basically an emotional, not a logical, process. For this reason a speech strategy based on audience interests is essential. Discover something the other person wants to do, be, or have; then connect what he wants to what you want, so that the action you are asking for will satisfy you both. The life insurance salesperson proves that your desire to safeguard your family can be satisfied, and at the same time satisfies her own desire to make a commission.

Be sure your motive is honorable. Persuasion is only a means to an end; it may be fair or unfair, honest or dishonest. It is your responsibility to be both fair and honest. An appeal based on sincerity and truth will have the best payoff in the long run. As Emerson puts it, "What you are stands over you and speaks so loudly I cannot hear what you say to the contrary." Not only can an audience detect a false approach, but life has a way of catching up with charlatans.

Give your credentials. Your strategic position will often be improved if you make sure that your audience knows enough about your background to judge the weight your words should carry.

Begin in a friendly way. Abraham Lincoln once said: "It is an old and true maxim that a drop of honey catches more flies than a gallon of gall. So with people, if you would win them to your cause, first convince them that you are sincere. Therein is a drop of honey that catches the heart; which, say what you will, is the great high road to their reason."

Be diplomatic. You don't persuade people to accept your ideas by stepping all over theirs; so handle controversial subjects with tender care.

Communication experts listened to 10,000 arguments of various kinds over a seven-year period. They came to the interesting conclusion that professional debaters, politicians, and United Nations delegates were less successful than door-to-door salespeople in getting their ideas accepted. Professional debaters try to beat down the opposition, whereas salespeople try to induce in their listeners an attitude of receptivity, wanting to change their minds. The experts found that the one big mistake most of us make in our attempts at persuasion is to attack the self-esteem of our listeners.

Use tact. No one likes to be told, "You're wrong." When you are trying to prove something, do it subtly. Begin by emphasizing those points on which you and your audience will most probably agree. Get your listener to say—or think—"Yes, yes" to a series of preliminary statements. Remember that when a person has once said no, his pride demands that he remain consistent.

Socrates originated the "yes, yes" technique. He would ask a series of questions with which his opponent would have to agree. Finally, almost without realizing it, his opponent would find himself embracing a conclusion that he would have bitterly fought a few minutes previously.

Don't imply that your opinions represent the final word. Instead of saying, "Certainly you can't deny" or "Undoubtedly this is so," preface your remarks with qualifications such as, "I believe" or "It appears." *A word of caution:* Don't use too many of these "softeners" or you will sound wishy-washy. State your case strongly, but take care to walk that thin line between confidence and arrogance.

Whenever possible, speak through third persons, such as an expert. A listener is naturally skeptical when you say things to your own advantage, so what a third source says is more likely to reduce resistance. Statements by authorities can be powerful, but quiet, ammunition.

When you are speaking with a small group, as in a staff meeting, there are additional persuasion techniques you can employ. The techniques that follow are effective in such situations because they allow you to discover the opinions of the listeners as you progress. There is, then, a chance for flexibility. In any less personal presentation, the only opportunity you probably will have for give-and-take is in the question-and-answer session that might follow your talk. Here are some "person-to-person" techniques.

- **Encourage the group to do a lot of the talking.** This is the best way to discover your listeners' backgrounds, interests, ambitions, and motives. By adjusting your persuasion to this data, you can increase your chance of success. Don't interrupt, even when you disagree: Your listeners won't pay attention to you as long as they still have something more to say. Remember, everyone loves a sounding board.

- **Don't force your opinions on your listeners.** Instead, make suggestions that let them think out the conclusion for themselves. No audience likes to feel they are being sold something or told to do something. They want to believe that they are buying of their own accord. If you allow your listeners to contribute to the plan of action, you are less likely to be turned down.

    Skillful persuaders almost always concede something. If you concede minor points, it's likely your listeners will more readily accept your ideas when you come to the major question. If possible, offer two alternatives for action, but be sure that both will accomplish your objective.

- **Seek a definite commitment.** Get your listeners' names on the dotted line immediately, while the conversation is still fresh in their minds. If you do get a ''no'' response, don't accept it as final; ask them to think it over.

The psychology of persuasion is a complex subject. As in every area of human relations, there are no rules; there is no ''pat'' answer or formula for using these techniques that will guarantee you success every time. But try them, and as you become more familiar with them, you will develop an awareness of the appropriate approach to take when faced with a variety of situations. Practicing these techniques will help you move toward your personal and business goals. Be sure what you are urging is ''right''—and then give it all you've got.

Chapter 9

SAYING WHAT YOU MEAN

You're listening to a speech draw near its conclusion and are waiting eagerly for the speaker to treat you to a dynamite closing. She says:

"Superscribe a dispatch to your duly constituted governmental authority eftsoons! Such a seasonable perpetration on your behoof will shroud your liberty and yellow boys!"

You shake your head, lost in a maze of meaningless words, your reaction being "Are you kidding?"

The speaker's closing remarks are, however, made up of good English words—they are just the wrong ones to get the meaning across clearly. A speaker must select the right word at the right time in order to communicate effectively. The translation of the above remark is: "Write your congressional representative today! Your prompt action will save you time and money!" Now we know what the speaker wants us to do!

When an artist sees an image he wants to paint on a canvas, he is faced with quite a task. First, he must acquire the proper brushes and colors. Then he has to apply these with skill and thought if he hopes to achieve a true reproduction of what he sees.

This same problem faces you when you have a thought you want to convey to others. You must be equipped with the proper words, and you must use them with skill and thought.

You should work continuously to improve your knowledge of the English language if you really want to say what you mean.

Basic Equipment: Words

First, look at your basic equipment—words. The English language contains well over 600,000 words and is by far the richest of all languages. And yet the average college graduate has a pitifully small vocabulary, broken down as follows.

- Our speaking vocabulary: 2,000 to 5,000 words

- Our writing vocabulary: 5,000 to 7,000 words

- Our reading vocabulary: 7,500 to 15,000 words

Do you really hold enough words, and the right words, to do justice to your thoughts and feelings? The extent of your vocabulary is often an index to your experience, background, interests, pursuits, and breadth of mind. You may be content with a few words, but do they really provide you with the equipment needed to dig up and express all those great ideas buried deep within you?

If you are not absolutely sure this is so, then involve yourself in a vocabulary-enrichment program. This is one area where assistance is plentiful but improvement is likely to be slow. Take your time and keep at it, using some of the following suggestions.

Besides an up-to-date dictionary, you can benefit from such books as a dictionary of American usage, a handbook of synonyms and antonyms, and a book of quotes and anecdotes. Don't leave your reference books on the shelf—use them. As you read and listen, refer to them when you encounter an unfamiliar word or usage. Become familiar with the origins of words by consulting your dictionary.

Broaden your reading habits. This is an excellent way to increase your word understanding. Be alert for new words; look them up, write them down, and try to find ways to add them to your vocabulary.

You can also do fun things such as buying a "word-a-day" calendar, working the "word-power" section found in many general magazines, attempting crossword puzzles, or taking up word-oriented board games.

You will be pleased with the results, as well as the increased enjoyment, you derive from communication. Do everything you can to give yourself the advantage when speaking, and you will find that you are more able to say what you mean.

The Choice of Words

In striving for better variety in your speaking vocabulary, ask yourself the following seven questions about any doubtful word.

- Is it a correct word?

- Is it used in the correct context?

- Is it exactly used?

- Is it simple enough?

- Does it have the right sound?

- Does it have the right "atmosphere"?

- Is it a spoken word, as opposed to a written word?

It's not essential that all these questions be answered in the affirmative. One requirement may sometimes need to be sacrificed for the sake of another that's more important. A word that is not necessarily correct may be used because of its adaptation to the listener or because of its atmosphere. A word that is not exact may be preferred because it is simple, and vice versa. Keep in mind, however, that if any word does not meet all these requirements, you should be able to justify your choice with sound reasons.

Denotation

Many large testing groups use vocabulary as one measure of a person's intelligence. It is also an indicator of one's ability to communicate with others. But just knowing a lot of words is not enough. It is important to choose the proper one to say what you mean. This choice depends on several things.

Each word has one or more definite denotations—it's literal dictionary meaning. The more you learn about these denotations, the more easily you can use the correct word and avoid common mistakes that range from selecting the absolutely wrong word to confusing similar words such as *effect* and *affect*; *insure, ensure,* and *assure;* or *imminent* and *eminent.* Learn to check the dictionary when you have even the slightest doubt or hesitation about the denotation of a word.

However, the problem of choosing words with the meanings you intend is not wholly solved by using a dictionary. You must also consider the level of your audience's understanding when you select a word. You could sound very educated if you use *lachrymose,* but more people would understand you if you said *tearful.* Keep the words you choose within the grasp of your audience.

And remember that words have different meanings to different people. *Heavy* might mean thirty pounds to an accountant and three hundred pounds to a weight lifter. With theatrical people, *heavy* refers to the villain in a play. So consider your audience when you select a word to carry the thought you have in mind.

Connotation

Each word also has a connotation—the suggestive significance it has acquired—apart from its explicit meaning. Because of their association with certain ideas they are commonly used to express, many words imply meanings not exactly expressed in the denotative definition.

What does the word *propaganda* mean to you? Most of us think of propaganda as material intended to deceive people about the true nature of something or to convince people that something is good when in reality it is not. We think of propaganda as "shaded" information that is manipulative and one-sided. More important, we think of it as the tool of "un-American," immoral, or cultist groups. That is the connotative meaning of *propaganda* for most of us. The denotative meaning is the spreading of any information intended to help or impair any person or cause, be it a political party, church, adoption agency, hospital, or health club.

Connotation is also determined by the "social standing" of a word, and how and when it is used. Some words belong in the street, some in the privacy of your home—but not in your presentation. Other words or phrases can have a different impact on different people. If you introduce yourself as a member of society's famous Four Hundred, you could create a favorable impression if there were other members present. To a nonmember, you would just appear snobbish. Get the desired reaction from your audience by considering the connotation of the words you use.

A carpenter has different types of hammers and tries to select the one designed for the particular task at hand. When you have an idea to drive home, words are your hammers. Choose the right one.

Use of Words

A Stradivarius violin will produce beautiful music when it is played properly. When used incorrectly, all you'll get out of it is squeaks and groans. Words are the same. Regardless of how carefully they are selected, they have to be correctly applied if you want to say what you mean.

The importance of being able to summon the right word at the right time has particular bearing on your ability to create interest. When choosing your words, remember to consider your listeners. Select the words that they will readily understand, and which will most effectively arouse their imagination.

Avoid using vague words—such as *gorgeous, magnificent, superb,* etc. Use concrete, imaginative words and phrases. For example, what does the word *loud* by itself convey to you? Combine it with *loud as a screaming jet,* and you now have a concrete picture. Likewise, *a large sum of money* lacks the impact of *$150,000. Home* conveys more than *house, golden* more than *yellow.* Select the exact word rather than the vague one.

Use clarity, conciseness, forcefulness, and good judgment when you put your vocabulary to work. Organize your words into logical sentences and paragraphs, and combine words so that they express clear thoughts. You can use figures of speech and examples where your meaning might otherwise be unclear.

Consider the background and knowledge of your audience, and remove or clarify any terms or expressions they might not know. This can be difficult. Expressions that are familiar to you and your work associates may be completely misinterpreted or misunderstood by listeners who don't do the same kind of work.

Select words and phrases that will most simply and clearly make your point. Say only what you must, and avoid superfluous statements. Be careful not to clutter your presentation with "nothing" phrases that simply take up time and water down your message. For instance, try not to use phrases such as, *I'd like to take this opportunity, If I may be permitted to say,* or *Let me summarize.* These are all easy to replace with more original and creative words—if you take the time to think about how you would rather hear it said if you were in the audience. Overused expressions will bore your audience; try to make it more interesting for both your listeners and yourself.

The way in which you apply your language can add forcefulness to the thoughts you express with it:

- Paint word-pictures that add spice, fun, intrigue, and power to your presentations.

- Create strong opening and closing statements.

- Use positive, rather than negative, words.

- Say *you, we,* or *us* rather than *I* as much as possible.

- Pick strong, descriptive words and phrases.

- Employ verbs that have life and motion.

- Avoid slang or profanity.

- Be conversational; use your voice to talk with your audience, not at them.

Chapter 10

TYPES OF SPEECHES

Prepared Talks

The term *prepared talk* means your presentation has been put together using a methodical approach similar to the one presented in this book.

Although a talk should never be memorized, you'll want to practice aloud enough so that your thoughts are firmly in mind. Brief portions of a talk that are direct quotations, or which must be precisely accurate in wording, may be read from your notes.

A prepared talk, then, is one that is planned in advance, practiced, and delivered conversationally and with as few notes as possible.

Impromptu Talks

The opportunity you have to speak before audiences large or small varies depending on your job, your outside interests, your personality, and your ability as a speaker. Whether the opportunities to speak in public are frequent or not, it's essential to be prepared when you get the chance. Success for you and the company you represent depends on your ability to make yourself heard by the right people at the right time. It is important to take advantage of the opportunity to talk whenever you can, to have something valuable to say, and to be able to say it effectively.

To express your ideas effectively at a moment's notice is an extremely difficult, yet important, challenge. The salesperson selling a product, the engineer describing a design, or the manufacturer proposing a production method invariably must speak spontaneously. The opportunity for an impromptu talk is present with every phone call, meeting, or conference. In fact, most business contacts are informal—times when your associates and your boss judge you on what you say and how you say it.

The impromptu talk differs from the prepared talk only in the amount of time available for planning. The normal prepared talk is thought out and rehearsed well in advance, but the impromptu talk must be organized and delivered almost simultaneously. Fortunately, the same steps used in preparing for an effective presentation can be applied.

First, determine your objective. When you're asked to comment on a subject, your first reaction may be to wish you weren't there. Your first ideas on the subject are probably not your best, but use them as a starting point in determining your objective. Be certain to establish your objective firmly in your mind as soon as possible, so your listeners will be able to stay with you.

Next, plan your strategy. There won't be much time, but remember to appeal to the interests of your listeners. These interests help you select what you should or should not say. Constant consideration of what appeals to the audience will keep you headed in the right direction. Think about previous comments the listeners have made; those will help you determine their interests.

The third step is to organize your ideas. In a prepared talk you would first think of a good attention-getter. In the case of an impromptu talk, however, this is a low priority. If you happen to think of a good opening when you stand up to speak, fine. But don't spend valuable time worrying about it. It's more important to get to the point quickly, tell your story forcefully, and conclude strongly. Your audience will forgive a poor start but not a poor finish.

It's rather like a very small boy riding a very large bicycle. As long as he keeps going, he's all right, but the only way he can stop is to fall down. This isn't a very impressive way to end a talk; so before you take a deep breath and take off on your bicycle, try to store away a good closing. Your audience may not remember the first words you speak, but they will remember the last.

There are a couple of ways in which you can develop your examples. You might relate personal experiences or work in a good story that illustrates a point. Or you might organize your examples in the "past-present-future" technique. Tell your audience how things used to be, how they are now, and how they should or will be. This method is particularly effective when you're discussing a new idea. It gives you the opportunity to develop your story to a logical conclusion and make recommendations.

Another approach is the "tell-'em-what-you're-going-to-tell-'em, tell-'em, and-tell-'em-what-you-told-'em" method. This works well for a descriptive or explanatory talk. It also gives you a little time to organize the details of your talk as you give your audience the general outline.

Above all else, keep your objective in mind constantly. If you should find yourself beginning to ramble, remembering your objective will bring you back to the point of your talk.

When you present an impromptu talk, you have no time for what would usually be the fifth step in preparation, evaluating your plan in advance. Evaluation is made on the spot by the listeners, and good audience contact will help you determine their reactions.

If you see their heads nodding in understanding or agreement, you're on the right track. If, however, the nodding is accompanied by half-closed eyes, you'd better add some dynamics before you lose them. If the reflection from your listeners is disbelief or controversy, you'll want to present additional examples or proof to serve as evidence in support of your point. Audience contact is of particular importance in an impromptu talk because it is the only way you can evaluate your performance. Keep your eyes on your audience!

For a prepared talk, the last step would be to practice. An impromptu also requires practice but in a different way. Obviously, you can't rehearse the particular talk you're going to present, but you can practice the art of impromptu speaking. Each time you talk, you should be thinking about and developing your impromptu skills.

Many of the techniques for becoming a good "ad-libber" are the same as for other presentations. Develop your voice so that you can speak clearly, forcefully, and with variety; learn to use natural gestures; and show your enthusiasm by putting expression into your face and voice. It doesn't make any difference if you are making a business presentation or telling a story . . . *be alive when you speak!*

Answering the telephone offers an ideal opportunity to develop your impromptu speaking techniques. When you are asked to answer a question, report on some activity, or comment on something, you are actually giving an impromptu talk. Use the principles of strategy and organization that you have already learned to make your telephone conversations successful.

Learn to think in terms of the preparation formula. Whenever you speak in a personal or business conversation, take a second or two to decide what you want to say, and how to say it. Remember, nearly every time you speak, you are presenting an impromptu talk. These can be either a daily chore or a daily pleasure. Make them enjoyable by learning to express your ideas effectively.

Manuscripts

Reading a paper is a very difficult way to make an effective presentation. Having a script with all the words right in front of you is dangerous because it is both too comforting and too confining. With everything down in black and white, you may have a false sense of security about the presentation and run the risk of falling into any number of the following traps.

- **You will probably sound as if you are reading.** From the listener's point of view, this means your voice will be monotonous, stiff, and dull. The principles of voice variety and forcefulness get lost in a script because what you are saying is coming from a piece of paper, not from you—your knowledge, experience, or feelings.

- **You will probably use awkward language.** There is a great difference between the way you would say something on paper and the way you would say it in conversation. As you write, you tend to be more formal, stilted, and involved in your phrasing. When you try to read these words aloud, you sound as if they came from a page of complicated encyclopedia text. You will sound unnatural, phony, and dull.

- **You may lose audience contact and stage presence.** With a complete script in front of you, your natural tendency is to glue your eyes on the page, keep your hands to the side of the lectern, and forget that there are people in front of you. Your personality disappears completely.

- **You may lose your place.** All those words in front of you can be very difficult to follow. If you lose your place—even once—while reading a presentation, you may panic and lose your control. Your carefully written speech can become a nightmare for both you and your audience.

Even with all these drawbacks, there are times when you may have to read from a piece of paper. Senior executives must do this a lot because exact, precise wording, approved by all authorities to safeguard against slips, is necessary to make sure that exactly the right thing is said in exactly the right way.

Even at lower levels, when extreme accuracy is important, speeches often must be read. If a speech is to be printed in a publication of some sort, the wording must be carefully screened to make it read as well as it sounds.

Sometimes when you use slides or visual aids in your talk, you may have to use a projectionist. If so, you'll have to use a script so that your assistant will know exactly when to project the next slide.

So there are times when you will be stuck with the task of reading a speech. Be prepared by knowing what the pitfalls are and how you can avoid them.

Effective Reading

Write the speech so it will sound good to the ear as well as look good to the eye. Sacrifice some of the fifty-dollar words that you looked up especially for the paper, and write it in language that is natural and conversational. As you write, read it aloud to yourself to determine whether or not it sounds natural.

Always have your speech typewritten on heavy bond paper (with an extra, clear copy for the projectionist if you are using one). Personal taste may vary on how a speech should be typed, but the following general rules have worked for most speakers.

- Type with double spacing between lines and triple spacing between paragraphs.

- Use a large, clear typeface.

- Type only on the right half of the page in a single column, similar to a magazine or newspaper. This is easier for your eye to follow.

Mark your script with reminders to yourself as to where to pause, where to speak more rapidly, where to emphasize certain points, and where to insert your carefully planned ad-libs. Other helpful hints may be:

- Underline important words or phrases.

- Use single slashes (/) to show minor pauses, and double slashes (//) to show major pauses.

- Use crescendo (>) and diminuendo (<) marks to remind you to vary the volume of your voice.

- Use notes on the left side of the paper to remind you to smile, relax, pause, use a visual aid, or whatever is helpful to you.

- Use phonetic spelling of words that may be difficult to pronounce.

- Use colored pencil, capital letters, or underlining to indicate where visuals should be used, marking these particularly on the projectionist's copy.

A sample script is shown on the following page.

Manuscript Markings

Relax	WHAT DO YOU FEAR MOST? IS IT HEIGHTS, / OR FIRE, / OR DEATH? // IN
Get Set	A SURVEY ASKING PEOPLE THIS QUES-
Eye Contact	TION, / *NONE* OF THESE WERE THE MOST COMMON ANSWER. // THE ONE MOST
Smile	OFTEN NAMED FEAR IS THAT OF PUBLIC SPEAKING. //
Remember	NOW, / HUMAN NATURE BEING WHAT IT
Eye Contact	IS, WE DON'T *USUALLY* LIKE TO DO SOMETHING THAT WE ARE DOWNRIGHT *TERRIFIED* OF. // SO WHY ARE WE WILLING TO STAND UP IN FRONT OF EACH OTHER / AND *TRY* TO SAY SOMETHING THAT MAKES SENSE? ///
Smile	WELL, / ONE OBVIOUS REASON IS THAT GOOD PUBLIC SPEAKING HELPS CAREERS. THERE'S *NOTHING* / LIKE FACE-TO-FACE COMMUNICATION TO GET A MESSAGE ACROSS. / PEOPLE WHO SPEAK WELL AT MEETINGS AND BEFORE GROUPS ARE SEEN AS MORE PROFESSIONAL / *AND* AS MORE COMPETENT.
Ad-lib	(USE EXAMPLE OF PERSONAL EXPERIENCE.)

Number the pages of your script clearly, and check the order before you get up to speak.

Don't staple the pages together. Keep them separate, moving each page to the side as you finish with it. Don't flip them over; just glide them directly to the side so that they are less distracting.

Don't fold your script unless you have to. Try to carry the pages in a flat notebook instead. If you have to fold them, do so opposite from the way you would fold a letter, with the typed side on the outside of the folds, not the inside. This will keep your script from closing up when you are trying to read from it.

Keep your script with you. Don't set it on the lectern *before* your turn to speak, or you face the danger of your introducer accidentally picking it up and taking it away! It's always a good idea to have two sets of notes for any number of unexpected "accidents."

Keep your head up and your eyes on the audience as much as possible. This is not as impossible as it sounds. By having the script typed clearly, you will be able to look away from the page much more frequently and keep eye contact with your audience. As an added precaution, put your finger next to the word you want to begin with when you look back down.

Take off your eyeglasses if you can see without them. Glasses will interfere with communication because they reduce the audience's ability to see your eyes, so you can lose some of the impact you want your speech to have. If you must wear them, try to choose a style that will allow your eyes to be seen as much as possible, and use nonglare lenses. Or you might choose to wear contact lenses instead.

While it can be effective to wear or remove eyeglasses at certain points for effect, try to wear them as little as possible. On the other hand, avoid getting into a routine of on-off-on-off: Because the visual element is such a strong factor, your audience will begin to count how many times you take your glasses off instead of listening to what you are saying.

Speak slowly and conversationally, maintaining your own personality in a natural way. Don't let yourself sound like a machine.

Use gestures. Mark your script as a reminder where you want to gesture, but don't plan any one specific gesture. Don't let your hands be glued to the lectern—let them go and they will naturally illustrate your words with appropriate gestures.

Stand straight, alert, and independent of the lectern. Don't hide behind it like a tombstone in a graveyard. As a variation, try setting the lectern at a slight angle and standing somewhat to the side of it. This will help the audience see more of you and will help you feel less chained to one spot. If you have planned some ad-libs, you can move forward toward your audience for those moments.

Practice, practice, practice. Become as familiar with the script as you possibly can without memorizing it. This will help you maintain eye contact, and vary your voice, gestures, and smile.

Remember, don't read a presentation unless you really have to. But if you must read it, prepare yourself and your script thoroughly. Practice it until you can deliver the speech as a truly effective presentation.

Technical Papers

You may be asked to present technical papers at meetings of professional societies. These papers are usually printed before or after the meeting, so there is no need to present all the details in your presentation. In fact, there are many reasons for not doing it.

The best one is that you will probably bore the audience to

death with a long, complicated technical dissertation. Remember, however, that only part of the audience may actually study your paper carefully when it is printed, and those who do not should be able to get all the major points by listening to you.

In this situation, you may want to use the following suggestions.

- Prepare your paper for publication with all the details in it.

- From this, prepare a condensed version you can deliver in ten to twenty minutes. Tell them simply what you did and why, then what results you found that are new and of interest to your audience.

- After familiarizing yourself with the condensed version, try a second condensation. Prepare a few notes and practice with them a couple of times. Then put them away and practice a couple of more times. Go ahead and get your notes if you need them, but try to practice until you can communicate the major points of your paper with a minimum of notes. Chances are that when you get up to actually give the presentation, you will have achieved a dynamic delivery, injected with your personality and excitement about the topic.

- Be prepared to support your main points more fully in a question-and-answer session. Chapter 13 will help you do this effectively.

Select the type of speech you will make based on your analysis of the audience and the situation. Then select the note format that will best allow you to communicate effectively with that group.

Chapter 11

CREATING THE RIGHT ATMOSPHERE

As you get up to speak, imagine yourself as a power-station generator. Electric power travels over the wires from the generating unit to the customers, connecting them to the source of power. In a similar way, you need to connect yourself—the source of power—with your audience. With your first words you throw the switch. The amount of power that travels from you to your audience depends on the way in which you use your natural personality to transmit your message. If your personality doesn't make contact with your audience, you are not going to get the results you want. But with your personality you can create a powerful surge of understanding and rapport, a connection with your audience that will make your message dynamic and memorable for your listeners.

To be successful, a presentation must not only be well organized and prepared according to the principles already discussed, but also must embody all of the many qualities that collectively make up its atmosphere.

Atmosphere may be defined as the group of qualities that increases receptiveness, creates understanding, relieves tension or hostility, and removes doubt or prejudice from the mind of the listener. The reaction of the audience to you and what you say depends directly upon the kind of atmosphere you create. Too often we are unconscious of the impression we actually do make upon others. Once you become aware of both the liabilities and—most importantly—the assets of your own personality, you can then begin to use it. Broadly speaking, atmosphere may be broken down into four areas:

- Personality
- The Human Quality
- Audience Contact
- Gestures.

Personality

Personality includes characteristics such as neatness, appearance, friendliness, humor, animation, voice quality, consideration, and imagination—to name just a few.

Personality is magnetic! But like a magnet, it can attract or repel. It's not only your greatest tool for holding the interest of your audience, it's the one factor that may cover a multitude of speaking faux pas. On the other hand, a perfect talk can be rendered lifeless by a speaker who has no spark or enthusiasm.

A charismatic personality can actually create in the listener a desire to be influenced. To be successful in persuading others, you must project the most attractive and appealing aspects of yourself as a unique individual. You need to create your own special "stage presence." Following are some suggestions on how to accomplish this.

Appearance. Choose your clothes with care. Taste and discrimination are essential in projecting the image that best suits your audience.

You will usually want to err on the side of conservatism rather than flamboyancy. Similarly, it's more acceptable to be slightly overdressed than it is to be too casual. How you dress is an indication of courtesy and respect, and should serve to put your audience at ease with you.

Be aware not only of style but also of color. While basic brown, gray, black, and dark blue are proper for some occasions, you'll want to wear brighter and less traditional colors for other settings. It's important that you look good but also that you feel good, so select something that is both appropriate for the audience and comfortable for you.

Be conscious of what jewelry you choose to wear, especially under stage lights. Choose a hairstyle that will stay out of your eyes and face, and only wear eyeglasses if you need them to see your notes.

Stance. Become familiar with what is known as the "ready stance": Place your feet about shoulder (armpit) width apart, relax your knees, and let your arms hang loosely at your sides.

This might feel strange at first because we don't normally stand this way. (A good place to practice it is in an elevator, or standing in front of the open refrigerator door!) This is your physical "anchor"; return to this position not only after taking a few steps or gesturing but also anytime you find yourself feeling a bit out of control. Pause, regain your stance, smile, and continue.

Posture. Walk, sit, and stand with your head up and shoulders straight. Stretch and relax tense muscles before you speak so that you look comfortable. Acquire a confident, courteous, alert appearance.

Poise. Quiet strength without nervous mannerisms shows self-control and commands respect. Your attitude should convey confidence and assurance, not hesitancy or uncertainty.

Gestures. When not in use, let your hands and arms hang relaxed at your sides. Don't glue them into your pockets or wave them around aimlessly. Keep them ready to use when needed, then use them with a natural definition and strength that exhibit conviction.

Practice hand and body movements, as well as facial expressions, that help you to communicate ideas. Using gestures also helps you to gain poise because a smooth, intentional movement helps to relax tense muscles while you talk.

Facial Expressions. Develop the habit of wearing a pleasant, bordering-on-a-smile expression. Develop a direct, interested look when you talk with people. A smile is a wonderful communication device!

Word Choice. Choose descriptive, colorful words that have life and stamina. Select words that enable your listeners to use their imagination freely. Paint effective word-pictures to illustrate your point. Be aware of words that give you a clue as to how they should be said, such as *smooth* (smoooooth).

Voice. Speak up! Enunciate your words distinctly, modulate your tone, change pitch, and vary the pace. Put emphasis and inflection into what you say.

Intentional Pause. Set off important phrases to allow sufficient time for a point to be absorbed. Pauses, without "uhs," lend atmosphere to a presentation and command the interest of the listeners.

The pause will give your listeners a moment to enjoy a memory you may have called to mind with a story, to experience the impact of a particularly powerful phrase, or to make a transition from one idea to another. In addition, it is one of the most effective ways to retrieve the attention of the audience if they have slipped away from you for some reason.

The Human Quality

To establish a common bond with your audience, practice—in your daily contact with others—those likable human qualities of interest, warmth, attention, sincerity, courtesy, and tact. This helps remove doubts, prejudices, and nervousness between you and your listeners. Following are some tips toward acquiring these qualities.

Friendliness. Develop a cheerful lilt to your voice. Wear a friendly smile. Keep a twinkle in your eyes. You are warm and human, just like your audience—show them! They will like you for it and be more receptive to your message. Learn to like people—then let your presentation style show it.

Courtesy. The basis of courtesy is kindliness—an attitude of putting yourself in the other person's shoes and a sincere desire to be helpful. Courtesy in speaking is essential if you want to influence others to your point of view. It is one of the basic elements of a pleasing and effective personality.

Tact. Closely allied to courtesy is the ability to exercise tact in all of your associations with others. It wins friends; the lack of it often loses them. Tact can be described as the avoidance of offense or unnecessary embarrassment to others. If you are tactless, you are being discourteous; if you exercise courtesy, you are being tactful.

It is very important to keep an open mind while you speak. We all resent condescension. We don't like being preached at, told what to do or not to do. We all like people who talk with us as equals.

Nothing will more effectively ruin a presentation than a superior attitude. Following are a few suggestions to avoid that problem.

Take responsibility for misunderstandings. Notice the "blaming" tone taken here: "I cannot see how you misunderstood." A more effective statement would be, "Apparently I did not make my meaning clear. . . ."

These two phrases both address the same problem—a breakdown in communication. The second one is not only more courteous but also illustrates a more positive approach to getting the communication back on track.

Suggest rather than command. Ask rather than order. Use commands very sparingly, even in your "call to action." A courteous command could be effective in that case, but it's usually better to suggest than to tell. It is sometimes necessary to issue very explicit orders; however, they should always be courteously worded. Contrast these two orders:

Poor: –"Arrange your schedule so that, without fail, you will be on hand for a conference to be held here on October 9. You must be present."

Better:–"It will be necessary for you to attend a conference to be held here on October 9. I would appreciate it if you would arrange your schedule so that you will be present."

The second is longer, but the length is justified because it doesn't leave a sting of brusqueness. It is—very plainly—an order, but it is a courteous one.

Request rather than order. The same request can be worded objectionably or courteously:

Poor: –You must complete the first quarter report by April 5. As you know, we were late last quarter, and it will not be tolerated this time. Call me if there are any questions."

Better:–"To assist the department in presenting our results to upper management, please have your first-quarter reports to me by April 5. If there are any questions, please give me a call."

Insist rather than threaten. Compare these two approaches:

Poor: –Coming in late is not acceptable. If this continues, it will lead to dismissal."

Better:–"To be fair to everyone and so that the workload is balanced, it's important that you are here right at starting time. I appreciate your understanding and cooperation."

Be sincere. Here is a closing statement that is so extravagant and overdone, it's disgusting:

Poor: –"It has been a really wonderful experience for me to share my thoughts with you today. Wherever you go, I hope you will always remember the importance of this message. Thank you so much for your attention."

Better:–"I enjoyed sharing some of my ideas with you today. (Pause) Thank you."

Audience Contact

As discussed earlier, if you wish to present an idea, you must establish contact with your audience by using an attention-getter and maintain that attention throughout the presentation. If you fail to establish audience contact, you are wasting your time and theirs; you will not accomplish your objective. Following are a few other critical elements of audience contact.

Eye Contact. You have all seen a successful speaker rise and, in that moment before he begins to talk, collect with his eyes the attention of the audience—including the woman in the fifth row who is examining her ring. This speaker captures their attention, then holds it by looking his listeners in the eye.

Eye contact is one of the most critical skills in being an effective communicator. Speakers often have difficulty with this because sometimes it seems easier to deliver a presentation if you don't look at anyone. It's true that all those eyes looking at you can be intimidating if you haven't learned how to use eye contact to your advantage and enjoyment, but ignoring your audience is no way to communicate with them.

If you want your message to be heard, you must use your eyes to make a connection with your audience. In our culture, eye contact is what tells us if someone really cares about the exchange taking place. Eye contact is also closely related to credibility: We have difficulty believing people who are not willing to look us in the eye when they say something. However, be aware that different cultures have other expectations regarding eye contact and its meaning. Careful analysis of your audience will help you be prepared for these differences.

The connection you create with your eyes is important to establishing a relationship with your audience. Think about what happens when you look at someone's eyes while you talk with them. There is an extra gleam of understanding because of the emotion people exchange with their eyes. Even if you happen to catch the eye of a stranger on a bus or walking down the street, you can't help but have an internal response.

Give yourself and your audience the opportunity to enjoy this exchange during your presentation. You can look people in the eye when you speak by talking to one person at a time for a moment or two, just as though you were in an individual conversation. Don't pick out a spot on the floor or ceiling and talk to that, and don't imitate a spectator at a tennis match by swiveling your gaze back and forth in long, sweeping glances. Instead, talk to one person at a time, and put your energy into looking not just at their eyes but into them.

Be careful not to talk to one person for too long, as that can be intimidating for your listener, and don't talk to the same few people over and over again.

When you learn to use good eye contact with your audience, you'll suddenly find yourself enjoying your presentation so much more. You will get an extra charge from seeing and communicating with the individuals out there instead of a sea of faces and eyes. You and your audience will be much more richly rewarded by a communication exchange made personal and dynamic by your ability to make the connection through good eye contact.

Interest. Audience contact can only be established if the audience is interested in you and what you have to say. If you try to present your subject with the interests and reactions of the listeners in mind, you are almost sure to accomplish audience contact.

This contact is maintained by both visible and audible means; the audience likes to receive with their eyes and their ears. Use a variety of facial expressions; life and animation together, with visible gestures. Give them variation in tone and pace, vocal animation, and conviction. If the subject warrants it, use demonstrations, charts, or pictures. Many uninteresting subjects have been turned into stimulating presentations by the combined energy of the speaker and exciting visual aids.

Enthusiasm. Conviction and enthusiasm are highly contagious. Through them you can tap the emotions of your listeners. Demonstrate to your listeners that you are convinced your idea is a good one. Make them feel you are compelled to let them in on it because it is too good to keep to yourself.

A presentation delivered in a dry, indifferent manner implies that you aren't really sold on its worth. Small wonder, then, if the audience agrees with you!

The best way to speak enthusiastically is to choose topics that hold some excitement for you. If you are really charged up about a topic, your nervousness will be transformed into enthusiasm and help you to transmit your convictions to your audience. So choose subjects that energize you, then let yourself go!

Gestures

A gesture is the intentional movement of the body to convey some thought or emotion, or to reinforce its verbal expression. Gestures are useful to:

- increase your energy and self-confidence
- assist in the communication of ideas
- help to hold attention.

But be warned: The impulse to gesture must come from within rather than from without. While you might use a cue in your notes to remind yourself that certain parts of your presentation would have more impact with gestures, you should never choreograph them. In other words, don't plan ahead that at a certain point in your speech you will make a certain gesture, since it will most likely look contrived and awkward.

Practice several gestures ahead of time, until you feel the natural swing of them. This will help you be more comfortable with a wide range of gestures, and they will appear naturally during your presentation.

Don't be afraid to let yourself go—just as the audience needs a lot of variation in your voice, they also need you to offer them visual variety by moving and gesturing to illustrate your words. Following are a few basic gestures.

Pointing (hand or finger). A motion like this is useful to call attention to objects or to a certain idea—but be careful about pointing at your audience.

Giving or receiving. This gesture uses open arms and hands with palms up. It suggests the giving of an idea or a request for support. You might use it to say, "I suggest you look at it this way" or "I urge you to accept this proposal."

Rejecting. This gesture uses open arms, palms facing the audience, like the gesture for *halt*. It expresses disapproval or rejection, such as, "This plan is not acceptable" or "It just can't be done this way." Use it sparingly! It can shut your audience out if used inappropriately.

Clenching the fist. Reserve this one for strong emotions, such as anger or determination. It might help you to say, "We've got to fight this one with everything we've got." Again, use it sparingly.

Dividing. Contrast or separation can be illustrated with this gesture. Simply move your hand from side to side either with the palm up or held vertically. This will help you make statements such as "neither radical nor ultraconservative" or "on the other hand."

Gestures are very effective tools for expressing emotion, as well as describing the size, shape, or motion of an object. Try showing the height of your sister by holding your hand in the air, or the speed of a car by a sweep of the arm. Other parts of the body can be used as well. You could use your legs to show how to kick a football or how your sister dances. Following are some characteristics of good gestures.

Vigor. Make them convincing. Avoid lazy, languid, ineffective gestures, especially when making a strong point. On the other hand, avoid the unintentional comedy of sledgehammering your fist into the table on minor points.

Definition. If you point to the window, make it clear and distinct. Avoid a blurred effect by running a number of gestures together or by using the same gesture repeatedly. Don't be jerky but, just as you need to enunciate words, enunciate your gestures.

Timing. The gesture should fall exactly on, or slightly preceding, the point it is used to emphasize.

In summary, you can create a favorable impression by combining the following invaluable personality characteristics.

- Watch your visual personality—appearance, stance, poise, gestures, and facial expressions.

- Listen to your audible personality—voice, diction, intentional pause, variation in pace and tone.

- Cultivate the human qualities of warmth, sincerity, friendliness, humor, courtesy, tact, and helpfulness.

- Achieve and maintain a connection with your audience through eye contact, interest, enthusiasm, and attention.

- Make your personality work for you!

Chapter 12

USING YOUR VOICE EFFECTIVELY

A mistake many speakers make is to say to themselves: "If I had that person's voice, I could be a terrific speaker too!"

Stop right there!

What makes a good speaker is not what voice you were born with, but what you do with it. While it's true that some voices are naturally more resonant than others, you can make your voice work more effectively for you by practicing techniques that will improve your vocal power.

The way you sound in speaking about a subject can sometimes overshadow the words you say. If you sound bored, listless, or unenthusiastic, your audience will probably feel the same way about your ideas. But if you speak forcefully and with enthusiasm, conviction, and variety in your voice, your audience will share the enthusiasm and be more eager to hear what you have to say.

Forcefulness

Your voice projects your personality to your audience. So how you apply forcefulness to your speaking will depend greatly on how you, as a person, normally think, speak, and act. But no matter what your normal style is, there are certain basic elements you must have if you are going to influence your audience favorably.

One of the key elements in forcefulness is volume. You must speak loudly enough so that everyone in the audience can hear you, but at the same time you must not shout at them. The secret is to control your voice strength. Developing the intensity with which you push your voice from your body by expelling air from your lungs is the first step toward achieving a forceful presentation.

How loudly you should speak depends upon the size of the room and the audience. Try to practice in the room in which you will be speaking by asking a friend to stand in the back and check your voice projection. If you can't do this, remember that speakers usually err by speaking too softly. Always speak to the person in the last row, not the first; the volume it takes to do this will not be too loud for the front row. If it is, you need a microphone.

A second key element of forcefulness is proper emphasis of important words and ideas. Although everything you say should be aimed toward accomplishing your objective, some facts, ideas, terms, names, statistics, emotions, results, etc., need to be emphasized. Varying volume at these points will help accomplish this.

To heighten the effect, you can use reduced volume in contrast with increased volume. As you speak more quietly, people tend to listen more closely, literally straining for your every word. But don't make your audience work too hard; even your softest words should be audible to the people in the last row.

Another technique that will give you greater emphasis is timing. The simple use of silence—intentional pauses—will impress your audience more quickly than an endless flow of words. The instant of silence before and after each key fact gives the audience a chance to absorb what has been said and to get ready for what is coming next. Surprisingly enough, the silence may even wake up that drowsy member of the audience who has been dozing—for the sleeper a pause can be more startling than an alarm clock.

More than just the use of pauses, though, timing depends on the rate at which you deliver your entire presentation. You may speed up to gloss over the less important words or to generate a sense of urgency or excitement. You may slow down to methodically spell out the things of greatest importance or convey the feeling of plodding, painstaking developments. Do both! Be sure your timing keeps audience interest focused on the key ideas and feelings that you want to convey.

Variety

Both volume and emphasis are important parts of the variety with which you speak. In the final analysis, variety makes the difference between boring your audience with a droning presentation or exciting them with a dynamic one. Unless you really want your audience to doze or think of other things, cultivate variety in your voice and avoid the monotonous, never-changing tone.

In addition to varying the volume and emphasis with which you speak, work for variety in your pitch and inflection. Learning to vary pitch is like learning to play a musical instrument. We first learn middle C, but to make music, we must master the rest of the scale. So it is with your voice. You have more range of pitch than you realize. Practice using it by literally talking up and down the scale. Raise your voice to a higher pitch to accompany the feeling of excitement, speed, or urgency. Lower it to the bottom of the scale where slowness, stealth, or even impending doom seem appropriate. Learn to use the full limit of your vocal range through practice, then apply it to make your voice more interesting to your audience.

Variety also depends on good inflection, or how pitch is

applied in a sentence. Statements of fact end with the voice falling to a lower pitch, whereas questions end with a higher pitch. The wrong inflection can make a serious statement sound funny, or can kill the punch line of a good story. Plan carefully to vary your voice to achieve the meaning you want.

Take, for example, the sentence, "I didn't say you are crazy." These six words can be pronounced in such a way that the sentence has six different meanings. Read the following aloud, stressing the italicized word.

- *I* didn't say you are crazy.   (But someone else may have!)

- I *didn't* say you are crazy.   (I absolutely did not say it.)

- I didn't *say* you are crazy.   (But I may have implied it.)

- I didn't say *you* are crazy.   (But I may have said your friend is.)

- I didn't say you *are* crazy.   (But maybe I think you soon will be.)

- I didn't say you are *crazy*.   (But I do think you are a little weird!)

Clarity

Perhaps the greatest problem speakers have—but one you can do something about—is enunciation. Since words are the tools of your communication skills, you must use them so that they will all be understood.

The only way to develop good diction and clear enunciation is to practice. Every time you speak, make full use of your lips, tongue, and jaw to form each syllable. Pay particular attention to the ending syllables, making sure you pronounce all the *-ings* and *-eds* correctly. In practicing, savor every syllable of every word as though it were a mouthful of good wine.

You can further develop good speaking habits if you practice reading aloud at home. Again, pay attention to saying every word as it should be said. Read at a natural pace and avoid slurring words together or blurring syllables by not forming the sound fully with your mouth.

Practice until good enunciation becomes a habit. It will pay off by making a more favorable impression on your listeners.

You can check your own progress by using a tape recorder. When you play it back, listen for the way you use your voice. Do you have adequate volume, variety, and clarity? Where can you improve? Then save the recording and try it again, working on achieving greater clarity. Record your practice session a second time, then listen to both versions. Have you improved? With the help of the tape recorder, you can make rapid progress toward improving the effectiveness of your voice.

If a tape recorder is not available, you can still evaluate your own voice. Simply cover up one of your ears while practicing. You'll find that you can hear your own voice more clearly with one ear closed than you can with both open. While this method doesn't permit you to evaluate and reevaluate as the tape recorder does, it at least gives you a rough idea of how you sound.

There are a few exercises you can use to help work on your diction and enunciation. First, open your lips only very slightly, and try to say *Ah*. It doesn't come out very well, does it?

Now open your mouth widely and say it again. Notice how much more clearly the sound comes out. Try the same exercise with the word *are*. You'll see that your lips are an essential part of good enunciation, because they form so many of our speech sounds. Notice how these words really make your lips work: *fool, food, owl, mouse, out, mum, pumice, poor*. Also try these words that make your lips stretch wide: *me, see, fee, tree, flee*. As you say the words, note how distinctness can be achieved by using your lips freely and energetically.

Practice with these and similar words until you are making full use of your mouth without effort. Then try putting the various sounds together into longer words, such as *mitigate, astronomy, geological*.

Here's a fun exercise in articulation. Try to pronounce each word of the following rhyme clearly but without seeming to make them painfully distinct:

> *A fly and flea in the flue*
> *Were lost—so what should they do?*
> *"Let us flee," said the fly;*
> *"Let us fly," said the flea—*
> *So they fled through a flaw in the flue.*

Vocal Exercises

There are several techniques for making greater use of your voice. Begin by acquiring flexibility of the muscles you use in speaking. These muscles need stretching so that they aren't tense or strained when you speak. Only relaxed throat and jaw muscles can produce full, clear tonal quality. The following exercises can help you relax.

The classic "let-it-all-hang-out" exercise. Yawn widely several times to relax your throat, tongue, mouth, and facial muscles. Then bend from your waist, letting your arms and the upper part of your body hang limply. Let all the tension drain out of those muscles. After a minute, raise your torso slowly. Repeat this several times. Then move your head gently from side to side until you feel the muscles of your face lose their tightness.

Throat massage. Begin gently just under your ears and slowly move down your neck. Loosen up your shoulder muscles too. This will help your vocal muscles become more relaxed.

Breathing. An important part of vocal control is breath control, or diaphragmatic breathing. Speech begins with expelling air from your lungs, not with contracting your throat muscles. If you expel all your air at once, the first tones will be fine, but the last ones will be weak and muffled.

Practice taking deep breaths, then exhaling slowly through your mouth. When you are really breathing deeply, you should be able to feel your stomach region push out. You can't stand stiffly and expect to breathe deeply.

Next, try exhaling while sounding a good, strong "Ho!" Be aware of using your diaphragm, not your throat, to supply the air for your voice. Then try two "Ho's," then several more in the same breath. Use this exercise to get the feel of allowing your diaphragm to support the sounds and conserve your breath.

After getting the feel of proper breathing, start saying a short sentence instead of "Ho." Use as many words as you can easily manage—contracting your stomach muscles slightly to push out each word. When you master short sentences, try longer ones, being careful not to use more words in one breath than you can manage easily.

Then try reading passages from a book or newspaper. Note the natural breathing places—usually found at punctuation marks—and then say each section in one breath with definite contraction of the muscles in your diaphragm. With a few weeks of this practice, you will be able to speak without any breath-control problems.

The following exercises are from Hoffman's *The Speaker's Notebook*, a delightful book on public speaking published back in 1943(!). Even if you aren't a poetry enthusiast, exercises like these can help you work on rhythmic breathing. To do this, read both passages in a chanting, singsong fashion. (These are also good exercises for practicing enunciation.)

> *Gold! Gold! Gold! Gold!*
> *Bright and yellow, hard and cold.*
> *Molten, graven, hammered and rolled;*
> *Heavy to get and light to hold;*
> *Hoarded, bartered, bought and sold,*
> *Stolen, borrowed, squandered, doled;*
> *Spurned by the young, but hugged by the old*
> *To the very verge of churchyard mold;*
> *Price of many crime untold—*
> *Gold! Gold! Gold! Gold!*
>
>   —Thomas Hood

> *Delaying and straying and playing and spraying,*
> *Advancing and prancing and glancing and dancing,*
> *Recoiling, turmoiling, and toiling and boiling,*
> *And gleaming and streaming and steaming and beaming,*
> *And rushing and flushing and brushing and gushing,*
> *And flapping and rapping and clapping and slapping,*
> *And curling and whirling and purling and twirling,*
> *And thumping and plumping and bumping and jumping,*
> *And dashing and flashing and splashing and clashing,*
> *And so never ending, but always descending,*
> *Sounds and motions forever are blending,*
> *All at once and all o'er, with a mighty uproar,*
> *And this way the water comes down at Lodore.*
>
>   —Robert Southey

Just for fun, try to repeat this one as fast as you can and for as long as you can: Red leather, yellow leather.

Resonance

Equally important in the production of good tone is proper resonance—the reverberant musical quality in the tone of the voice. Some voices are naturally richer in quality than others, but unless there is some impairment of the palate or larynx, any voice can be made pleasing and expressive.

Try the following exercise and see if it doesn't help you. Close your mouth and hum for a moment. Feel the vibration in the sinuses and the forward part of your head? Practice by starting to hum—"Hmmmmmmmmmmmmm"—then, without a pause, work into "sing . . . thing . . . bring." Keep the *ng* sound going all the time. Work from humming into speaking, trying to keep the tone up in front and the vibration in the nasal cavities.

To further develop resonance, read aloud the following exercises, again from Hoffman's *The Speaker's Notebook*. Try to use a full range of pitch and volume as you read them aloud.

- Nine unknown men in Maine.

- Boomlay, boomlay, boomlay, boom.

- Mee mee mee mee mee mee mee mee.

- Ming ming ming ming ming ming ming.

- Hum and intone more morning songs.

- Roll on, thou deep and dark blue ocean—roll!

- He sinks into the depths with bubbling groan, without a grave, unknelled, uncoffined, and unknown.

Once again, poetry can be a good way to practice using your voice effectively. The following short poems might work for you.

Solemnly, mournfully,
Dealing its dole,
The Curfew Bell
Is beginning to toll.

      —Longfellow

Up! Up! my Friend, and quit your books!
Or surely you'll grow double;
Up! Up! my Friend, and clear your looks;
Why all this toil and trouble?

      —Wordsworth

If poetry isn't for you, try reading from a brochure about a place you would like to visit, a sports magazine, or whatever material strikes your interest. Be sure it is something you like, or you'll have a tough time reading with expression. Choose something you can get excited about!

Only one rule holds the secret for all voice improvement—practice! While you never will have the voice that someone else has, you will increase the effectiveness of your own. Here is an excellent speech for practice, as well as for the ideas it contains.

Hamlet's Instructions to the Players

"Speak the speech, I pray you as I pronounced it to you, trippingly on the tongue. But if you mouth it, as many of our players do, I had as lief the town crier spoke my lines. Nor do not saw the air too much with your hand, thus, but use all gently; for in the very torrent, tempest, and, as I may say, whirlwind of your passion, you must acquire and beget a temperance, that may give it smoothness. O! It offends me to the soul to hear a robustious periwig-pated fellow tear a passion to tatters, to very rags, to split the ears of the groundlings, who for the most part are capable of nothing but inexplicable dumb shows and noise. I would have such a fellow whipped for o'erdoing Termagant. It out-Herods Herod. Pray you, avoid it.''

—Shakespeare

Microphones

You will need to learn to work with a microphone for many speaking situations, since it can project your voice outdoors and in large meeting rooms. Unfortunately, a microphone also has a tendency to underplay your normally good speaking qualities. After learning to use your voice properly, you need to learn a few additional techniques to get the most out of a public-address system.

While many facilities will have up-to-date equipment that will give you few problems, many others will be ill equipped. Be sure you find out ahead of time what kind of system you will be using.

Single-directional microphones are difficult to use because you must speak directly into them at all times. You will be misunderstood and not even heard if your voice fades and booms erratically. Control of your body movement will help you maintain a constant distance from a stationary mike. If possible, arrange for a hand-held or clip-on mike. This will help you maintain constant volume yet still move around. Use the microphone as you would a telephone, speaking into it directly and clearly.

Omni-directional microphones are much easier to use. You

need not worry about keeping your mouth practically glued to the microphone during your entire talk. You will, however, need to keep the following points in mind.

Speak a little more slowly than usual. Your normal delivery is probably too rapid for a public-address system. The words tend to chase each other, and this is confusing. Each word must have a chance to be heard.

Control your breath. Breathing errors will be exaggerated. Horrible gasps and wheezes can be eliminated if you plan your pauses and breaths. A quick, quiet technique for breathing is similar to yawning. Arch your tongue tightly against your lower teeth, then, with your jaw relaxed, simultaneously open your mouth quickly, force your diaphragm out, and draw in your breath. Then, like a singer, phrase your talk for optimum breathing smoothness.

Enunciate clearly. Similar sounds lose definition, so enunciation must be even more precise than in normal speech. Certain sounds, however, whistle and hiss because of the high pitch needed to voice them. Sounds such as *th*, *s*, *z*, *sh*, *v*, and *t* can be softened by cutting them off short after making them.

Be conversational. The public-address system plays down your vocal variations because there is now an electronic device between you and your audience. Greater variety is needed to maintain audience attention.

Stand clear. Adjust the microphone so that it is below, not in front of, your face or you'll lose audience contact. Avoid tapping the lectern, rustling the pages, or other distractions. If it is a "gooseneck" microphone, switch it off to adjust it. This will eliminate that horrible metallic shriek. Just remember to turn it back on again!

A tape recorder can help you evaluate your use of the microphone, as can a friend who is willing to listen to your practice. Be sure you arrive at the place where you will be speaking early enough to practice with the system available so that when the audience arrives, you won't lose credibility by looking like you don't know what you're doing. Keep the above points in mind, use your natural voice, and practice!

Chapter 13

QUESTIONS, QUESTIONS, QUESTIONS

There are many ways to use questions as part of your presentation besides in a question-and-answer (Q&A) session at the end. During your talk, questions help to keep the audience involved in your topic at a personal level. Here are a few ways in which you can do this.

Rhetorical Questions

Rhetorical questions can be a great tool for putting the audience in the frame of mind you want them in to hear your message better. It differs from an interactive question in that you don't want the audience to answer you, only to have an internal "uh-huh" or "oh-yeah" response. Another use of the rhetorical question is to gain the attention and interest of the audience or to introduce your subject, such as, "Would you like to make a million dollars?"

Rhetorical questions are tricky because, while you may use the very same words as in an interactive question, by your delivery you're indicating to the audience that you don't actually want an answer. Your voice and manner must tell them that you are using the question as a statement. The pause after the question will be shorter, and you may even answer the question yourself.

Practice delivering your rhetorical questions into a tape recorder to evaluate your use of inflection and pitch. Practice pausing long enough for the audience to process the question, but not so long that they think they should respond. But beware—no matter how skillful you are at delivering the rhetorical question, there is always a strong possibility that someone will throw out an answer; when you plan a rhetorical question, practice how you will handle the clown who does!

Interactive Questions

There are many ways to use a question to which you really do want an answer. Following are a few.

Ask for a show of hands. A common practice is to ask the audience, "How many of you . . . ?" If you do this, you need to signal your audience that you want a response by raising your own hand, or even by saying, "I'd like to see how many of you . . . Could you put your hands up, please?"

Then it is important to reflect back to the audience how many responded: "I can see that most of you . . ." or "I see that just a few of you . . ." This is important because human nature is to be curious about how we "measure up" to each other. It's your responsibility to be sure the people in the first few rows get the same information verbally that everyone else gets visually.

A pitfall in using this technique is that you won't always get the answer you want. If your next statements are based on the assumption that 75% of your audience will respond affirmatively, and only 25% do, you have a problem. You need to plan several "next statements" for whatever response you get. Part of this can be taken care of in your audience analysis stage, but not always.

Suppose your talk is about the fears employees have during a time of corporate change; you might plan to begin with an analogy of some other common fear of, say, flying, heights, or public speaking. You might start by asking, "How many of you are afraid of . . . ?" If most of the audience raises their hands, you can say, "I see that most of you can identify with this fear. Corporate change is also frightening. . . ."

If, however, only a few people raise their hands, then you'll have to say something like, "How many of you are more afraid of heights?" (A few more hands.) "How about public speaking?" (More hands.) "You can see that we all have fears about different things. Those anxieties are not much different from what we are experiencing as our workplace changes."

When you do this, don't let anything in your voice or manner show that the audience didn't give you the answer you first wanted. If you do, they won't want to cooperate with you because they don't want to be "wrong."

Writing audience answers. Asking questions and writing the audience's suggestions on a flip chart, overhead transparency, or chalkboard is especially effective in a small group or staff meeting. It can create a "picture" of the group's ideas. This is an easy way to build a sense of closeness or common concern within a group.

By the way, if you inadvertently misspell words when you're using this technique, don't apologize or waste time trying to fix it; let your audience enjoy your willingness to be human and make mistakes. But don't be gimmicky and make a mistake on purpose.

Open-ended questions. Allowing audience members to share their own stories, experiences, ideas, and concerns can be very effective and a lot of fun. It takes a great deal of skill to manage an open session like this, so don't attempt it with emotional topics until you have developed some expertise. It's also more difficult to stay within time restrictions with open questions, and they leave the audience an opening to move the discussion away from your objective.

Question-and-Answer Sessions

Q&A usually takes place at the end of a presentation. There are two common ways to move into a Q&A session. One is to close your presentation with your "results" statement, pause, and invite the audience to question you. The second is to speak for only a portion of the time allotted, and without any formal transition, say, "How does that plan sound to you?" or "How does this fit with your experience in this area?"

The latter technique is usually only effective with small groups but can be a good way to get the listeners involved in a more open discussion instead of just listening to you and then asking a few clarifying questions. It's also a good way to evaluate your audience's needs on the spot. You know you will be addressing what they want to hear, because they are providing you with the clues you need in their questions. Whatever approach you take, you will need to keep in mind the following guidelines.

Prepare. Imagine the questions that you might be asked, and think through the answers to them. You might ask a colleague to listen to your presentation and ask questions so you can be prepared for the person in the audience who knows as much about the topic as you do.

Prepare for receiving no questions. If this happens, don't say, "Well, either I did a really good job or I totally confused you." Worn-out phrases like this will destroy everything you accomplished in your presentation. Instead, simply say, "In closing, then, I would like to remind you . . ." and finish with a brief restatement of your results.

Listen. Listen to the entire question with a calm, interested expression and with good eye contact. Don't look away to think about the answer before you get the whole question. Eye contact is an important sign of attention; don't diminish the credibility you so painstakingly built up in your presentation by losing your audience connection in the Q&A.

Think before you speak. An answer is a short presentation and requires a moment of preparation. Pause to gather your thoughts so you can be sure you are answering the question, not talking around it. Even if you know the answer immediately, it's a good idea to pause before you answer. This tells the questioner you are really concerned about giving the correct answer, not a pat one.

Think in silence. Avoid fillers, such as, "That's a good question" or "I'm glad you brought that up." Just as the opening of your presentation should be clean, you don't want to make a false start before answering.

Be direct. Put the answer up front, even if it is simply yes or no. Provide a deeper explanation only if you are asked for it. In other words, don't answer the unasked question. Your answers should be thirty seconds or less. If the audience wants to know more, someone will ask.

Answer the whole audience. Look at the questioner to begin your answer, then move your eye contact around to keep everyone involved. Don't go back to the questioner at the end of the answer, or you could wind up inviting this person into a private conversation with you. If necessary, the questioner will ask another question later on.

Be willing to say "I don't know." You can best maintain your credibility by being honest about not knowing the answer. Do offer to find out by inviting that person to see you after the presentation. If you say, "I'll get back to you on that," be sure you do.

Diffuse hostility. There are times you will be speaking on controversial topics and get angry questions. You need to learn not to take this personally. Listen to the person's question and feelings while they talk, then acknowledge the emotion before you answer. This can be done with any number of phrases, but be sure you choose one that is sincere for you. You might try some of the following.

- I can understand why that would make you angry.

- I know, I get angry about that too.

- A lot of people share your feelings.

- It is very frustrating to be in your position.

Then, just answer the question. Don't respond to the emotion any further.

Repeat the question. There are times when you won't need to do this, but often you will, if the whole audience can't hear the question or if someone asks a long, rambling question, for example. In this case, you would want to repeat it in a clear, condensed version. It is also a good idea to repeat a hostile question without the accompanying emotion; simply restate it in calm, positive terms.

Acknowledge statements. Often there won't be a question; the listener is using the question-and-answer session to state a point of view. All you need to do is thank the person for the idea. "Thank you for mentioning that" or any similiar phrase will do. Follow it with, "May I take another question?"

Stay on the subject. Sometimes your audience will want to move away from your objective and turn the session into a forum for another topic. It's your responsibility to keep things on track by saying something like, "That's a subject I'd really like to spend some time on, but right now I'd like to get everyone's questions about (topic)." An exception would be if you are knowledgeable on the subject and can answer briefly.

Close with your objective. Don't let your presentation trickle to an end or close with a question somewhat distant from your objective. When you are out of time, or there are no more questions, you need to make a closing statement that leaves your "results" in the mind of the listeners.

Prepare yourself mentally ahead of time, following these guidelines. You'll find that questions can be an exciting part of your presentation.

Chapter 14

VISUAL AIDS

Alex Osborn suggests: "Put some spin on your idea . . . take it out of the humdrum and make it easier to grasp."

Fact is, the eye is twenty-two times as powerful as the ear in transmitting responses to the brain. Whenever possible, add the visual element. This might be as simple as a pad and pencil in a conversation, or as elaborate as a multi-image audiovisual presentation in a theater filled with hundreds of spectators.

It is of critical importance to accompany your verbal message with a visual one. While sometimes the visual will be you—your facial expressions, gestures, and movements—it could also be some type of graphic medium. The following illustrations shed some light on why this is so important.

A dynamic delivery is one that involves your audience totally. Note the following chart describing how people absorb information:

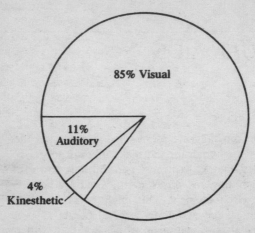

(From a study by Columbia University)

In addition, people's recollection (one week later) of presentations with a variety of styles is shown in this graph.

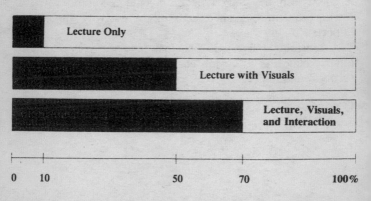

(From a study by Dr. Elizabeth Fletcher, University of Arkansas)

The point: For impact—and to be remembered—use visuals.

You could spend the next thirty minutes using words to describe a friend of yours. You could do the job in an instant if you showed a photograph of her. Research has shown that your audience will retain more of what they see in the picture than they will from your words. Apply this principle to every presentation you make. Most importantly, remember that you, yourself, are a visual aid. Use your face, gestures, and movements to illustrate your words and make the work of understanding your presentation easier for your audience.

Where Do You Begin

A simple definition of a visual aid is any visible device used to clarify the message you are presenting. So begin by looking for those parts of your presentation that could be told more effectively with some visual assistance.

There will be many occasions when visual aids will help you, but beware of a major pitfall: The visual must never be a crutch; it must always supplement your talk, and you must always be the center of attention. Plan visuals to simplify a talk, keep the number to a minimum, and resist the temptation to build a talk around an existing visual. A good visual will:

- be easily seen and heard

- support a clear verbal message

- serve the objective

- be simple (one unit idea)

- have impact—and get the message across

- reflect quality and pre-thought

- be rehearsed (at least three times).

Selecting Visuals

Once you find a need for a visual, select one to do the job. You may want to get advice from various people with expertise in this area. They can help you determine and develop whatever might be most appropriate—video, slides, overhead transparencies, models, flip charts, etc. But most often you will have to prepare simple aids using the tools at hand. To help you determine which visuals may be appropriate for a variety of situations, refer to the following chart.

Visual Aids

Aid	Lighting	Expense	Additional Equipment	Audience Size*
Prepared easel chart	On	Low-high	Stand, Projector	Small
Blank easel chart	On	Low	Stand, markers	Small
Slides	Off/dim	Med-high	Projector, screen	Small–large
Overhead Transparency	On/dim	Low-med	Projector, pens	Small–large

Aid	Lighting	Expense	Additional Equipment	Audience Size*
Movies	Off	High	Projector, screen	Small-large
Video	On/off	High	TV set, playback	Small–medium
Chalkboard	On	Low	Chalk, pointer	Small
Print photos	On	Med-high	Photo service	Small–medium
Handouts	On	Low	Copy service	Small–large

*Audience Size:
   Small—1–20
   Medium—20–50
   Large—50–1000 +

Creating Visuals

Build a simple, inexpensive visual-aid kit so you'll be prepared at all times: a large easel and pad; several pieces of poster board; some large, colorful felt markers and chalk. Never overlook the usefulness of a plain pad and pencil in an office conversation—the visual aid is anything that will help illustrate your idea. You are limited only by sheer practicality in some cases, but for most presentations, you can let your imagination run free. Your audience will enjoy the flavor you have given your talk, and so will you.

Visuals needn't be either expensive or professionally developed to be effective. One ounce of imagination is far more valuable than a lot of expensive, but dull, visual aids. Following are a couple of quick ways to evaluate the visual you have created.

The ABCD Rule	The 4B Rule
Appropriate	Big
Big	Bold
Clear	Bright
Different	Brief

Visuals prepared either in advance or "as you go" during the presentation must be easily read. Following is an example of an overcrowded visual and how to simplify it.

Overcrowded	**Better**

Three Keys to Delivering An Effective Presentation	*Three Keys*
• Always speak in an area of your strengths.	• Strengths
• Do a thorough audience analysis.	• Audience Analysis
• Infuse your presentation with personal energy.	• Energy
These are your keys to greatness in speaking.	

One method that is especially effective for slides but is also useful for flip charts or overhead transparencies, is the "reveal method." Below is an example showing the three keys to making an effective presentation.

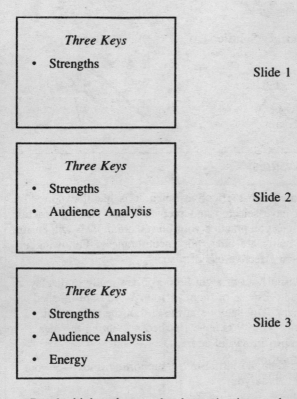

People think and remember better in pictures than in words. As often as possible, use a "pictograph," or illustration, to support your points. Here are a few examples, created by Jennifer Hammond Landau and Jean Westcott.

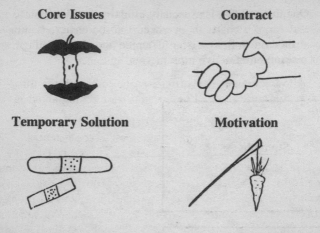

Core Issues

Contract

Temporary Solution

Motivation

Using Visuals

Any visual is most effective when it is handled correctly. After you have selected and prepared your visuals, practice using them as you practice your presentation. This will ensure that they really are aids, not encumbrances. Following are some tips on effective use of visuals.

- Keep visuals out of sight until you are ready to display them, and dispose of them as soon as you are finished with them. This may be at the end of the talk, but it is usually when you have finished presenting the idea or example the visual addresses.

- Always keep the visual in a "supporting role"—at your side or behind you.

- Maintain constant eye contact with your audience so that they will know you are at center stage, and that they should return their full attention to you as soon as they have absorbed the visual.

- Avoid looking at the visual any more than absolutely necessary while you are talking; if you have to handle it or write something on it, stop talking until you can return your full attention to your audience.

- Allow the audience sufficient time to absorb the information on the visual before you start talking about it.

- Don't stand directly in front of the visual unless you want to gain the complete attention of the listeners.

Get a lightweight sports bag and make yourself an "emergency kit" containing everything you'll need to bail yourself out of a possible jam. This kit would include extra projector bulbs, an extension cord, a variety of electrical adaptors, marking pens, a collapsible pointer, extra three-by-five cards, masking tape, thumb tacks, paper clips, chalk and chalk holder, sewing kit, etc., etc., etc.

If you have difficulty imagining what you could possibly need all these items for, just think of all the things that could go wrong with the arrangements you've made for a presentation. If you still can't think of why you would need this or that, pack them, anyway. It's a sure bet that one day you'll be glad you did!

Check the room in which you will be talking to be certain that there are adequate facilities for the visuals you will be using. Pay particular attention to the electrical outlets and their location. Be certain that you have a well-trained operator if you are going to need assistance with film or slide projectors. And have someone prepared to operate the lights for you. You might try to arrange for a dimming switch on the lights so that you won't subject your audience to severe light changes. Arrange your stage area so that you can move to your visuals easily, and that they present a pleasing environment for your talk.

In general, just remember to be considerate of your audience. Remember that the visual is to help tell your story, so use it in a manner that will make it a real asset in the eyes of your audience. Never take your visuals for granted—practice using them so that they will blend smoothly and usefully into your presentation.

Slides, Overheads, and Flip Charts

While all of these can add clarity and excitement to a presentation, they can also be detrimental.

Using slides usually requires more darkness than overheads, and it is too easy to lose the eye contact you need to get your message across on a personal level.

While overheads can be used with less darkness, it is too much of a temptation to use transparencies duplicated from black-and-white typewritten pages. This is terribly dull and tells your audience that the message is probably boring too. You will have a tough time convincing them otherwise. Instead, take advantage of current technology to create bold, colorful transparencies to accompany your message. Or make them yourself with the colored pens designed for the medium. Even hand-drawn visuals using color are better than black-and-white typewritten ones.

Flip charts are best utilized if they are prepared in advance but are only effective for relatively small groups. Beware of putting more than one idea on a chart and of writing too small. If you have a lot of data you want to back up with visuals, too many flip charts could be difficult to manage well.

Regardless of the medium you choose, be sure that all your visuals are in the right order and marked clearly so that if they should happen to be dropped, they can be reordered quickly and accurately. This is especially true for slides— number them all on the same side so they can be faced correctly. Keep the following hints in mind as you practice with your visual aids.

Visuals must be appropriate. Be sure that all your visuals relate directly to your objective, or the result you want.

Visuals need not be used during the entire presentation. A thirty-minute speech might include only five minutes of slides or overheads, and a twenty-minute talk might only need one flip chart. Remember that a visual should always help, not hinder, you as the focus of your presentation.

If a visual needs a preliminary statement, make it before the image or chart is shown. Then reveal the visual and, if necessary, explain it more thoroughly.

Allow the audience a moment to look at the visual before talking about it. When about three quarters of the audience is looking back at you, they have absorbed the visual and are ready for you to continue. (These pauses are good moments to silently take a deep breath and relax.)

Finish your comment on a visual and then remove it from view. Say nothing more about it except what may be necessary to link it to the next visual or idea.

Similarly, don't begin to comment on the next visual until you have shown it to the audience and allowed them to look at it for a moment. When practicing and timing your presentation, remember to build in these moments or you will not be able to remain within the allotted time frame.

Leave your visual in view long enough to do its work, for its significance to sink in. Make the most of it and don't hurry through it, but don't overuse it, either.

Leave the screen or easel empty between visuals by using a blank page between flip charts, solid plastic "blackout" slides, or a piece of cardboard on the overhead surface. You could turn the projector off between transparencies, but this can be distracting if you turn it on and off too much.

Stand on the same side of the screen or easel for each

visual. Move from side to side occasionally for variety but only in between—not during—your visuals.

Don't make aimless body movements such as jerking your head toward the visual while talking about it or handling it too much.

When using flip charts, you may want to write lightly penciled notes to yourself on the edge of the paper. If you use this method, however, be sure the notes are a reminder, not everything you want to say. Glance at them to get your thoughts, then return your eyes to the audience.

If your flip charts are prepared in advance and you need to roll them up to transport them, roll them with the graphics on the outside. While you may think this is backward, it will prevent the bottom of the sheets from rolling up like a window shade when you are trying to use them. A good way to transport them is in a cardboard mailing tube.

Chalkboards and Whiteboards

Chalkboards are difficult to use effectively because many people can't read them unless they are sitting in the first few rows. Even with colored chalk, reading a chalkboard can be hard work for your audience, especially if you have erased a couple of times. You also face the danger of inadvertently turning your presentation into a comedy routine by getting chalk on your clothes, your face, everywhere!

A better option is the white melamine "greaseboard" that you can use bright markers with. The contrast between the white background and the colored ink makes it easier to read. A whiteboard can be erased and used over again just as easily as a chalkboard, and it eliminates the turning of pages required by a flip chart. Just be careful to use the special "dry-ink" pens made for this kind of a surface—most of the markers you would use on a flip chart will not wipe off the whiteboard.

Using a Pointer

A pointer is used to draw attention to a specific place on a visual.

For slides, use a long pointer so that you can reach entirely across the picture without casting a shadow on the screen or interposing your body in front of the frame. If you are using overheads, use a thin, short pointer to indicate items by placing it on the projector face itself, not pointing to the screen. This will allow you to remain facing your audience, not turning your back on them to point.

A pointer is useful for flip charts as well. In this case, use a pointer that is long enough for you to stand slightly away from the charts, so that you don't interfere with your audience's line of vision. Don't reach across your body to point: stand to the left and use your right arm, or vice versa, so that your arm extends comfortably away from you. Be careful to use the pointer only to indicate, not as a crutch. Have the pointer within easy reach, and have a place to put it when it is no longer needed. Avoid the following distractions:

- the dueler

- the parade-rest stance

- the orchestra leader or the baton waver

- the tapper

- the leg scratcher

Video

Using video in a presentation can be very exciting because it can add color, motion, and sound at the same time. If you choose this medium, be sure you arrange for video equipment that is compatible with your tape. Check the equipment ahead of time to ensure that it is in good working order. If you don't know how to operate it yourself, arrange for a technician to be on hand to troubleshoot.

One difficulty with video is having a monitor large enough for everyone to see. While big-screen TV is a big help, it may not be readily available. You can set up more than one monitor instead, but you'll need a technician to set them up so that they are synchronized.

As with any visual aid, remember not to talk during its use. If you want to comment on a picture, shut the sound off. It will also help to be sure all the cords are well out of your way so you don't trip on them!

Exhibits and Samples

A presentation that involves the use of actual exhibits of material is the easiest of all to give, and it's one that is most likely to please the audience. Demonstration of statements by concrete objects appealing to the senses—sight, smell, touch, taste, and hearing—is a highly successful way of telling your story.

However, unless they are used properly, exhibits and samples can interfere with and destroy your presentation. Following are a few hints to help make this approach successful for you.

• Conceal the exhibit, sample, or prop until your discussion calls for it.

- If an exhibit is large and cannot be concealed entirely, then at least cover it to keep it in the mental background of your audience. Add pizzazz to your presentation with little things. Cover your props with a cloth or hide them in the lectern shelf until you need them. Practice removing the cloth with a flourish at just the right instant, or bringing the hidden prop into view gracefully.

- If something is to be examined by the audience, give them a chance to do this at the time you begin talking about it. (Remember the time factor!)

- Don't distribute samples unless you have enough for everyone, and don't talk while distribution is taking place.

- When holding up a sample, hold it at your side at about shoulder level and in full view of the audience. Keep your attention on the audience, not the sample. You already know what it looks like, so keep your eyes ahead.

- An exhibit that you can demonstrate or which has moving parts is more dramatic than a static one. If it is appropriate, build a "living" prop into your talk. Again, be sure to practice with it so your motions are professional and your timing rehearsed.

- Above all, any exhibit worth doing is worth doing well. Be professional in your choice and handling of any supplement to the spoken word.

Reference Material

Handouts are sometimes a very useful visual aid. They can also be the number-one killer of a potentially great talk. There is nothing worse than your audience burying their noses in paper while you are trying to communicate with them. As with slides, you lose the opportunity for the eye contact you need to deliver a message well.

It is true that some informational or instructional talks need reference material along with the spoken word to help make the message more clear. If that's the case in your talk, following are some suggestions for the effective use of handouts.

If you will not be actually discussing the material in any depth, or the audience does not need it to understand your message, it should not be made available until you are finished. It can be distributed after you close, or placed on a table for the audience to pick up as they leave. In either case, refer to the material and how to get it only at the end of your talk. Avoid referring to the material earlier in your talk, or your audience will feel that there is no need to listen to you.

Material to be distributed should be on hand and in sufficient quantity. If you forget to bring the material or it is not available for some reason, don't say so. Never tell your audience what they are missing.

If the handouts are needed at the very beginning, they should be distributed before the speech has begun. Place the material at the table or on the chair of each person before anyone arrives.

When the material is not needed until later on in the talk, it should be distributed just at the moment you will address it. Have someone prepared to help you with this so that you don't step out of your role as speaker and into that of assistant. Or, hand the material to one person on each side of the room and ask them to pass it around. Whatever method you use, don't talk again until the material has all been handed out and your listeners have had a chance to look it over. Give them time to satisfy their curiosity before you go on.

There is nothing wrong with giving your audience instructions as to when to look at the material and when to put it away. If you are working with the handouts during your talk, it is a courtesy to tell your listeners what page, paragraph, chart, etc., to look at. Make it as easy as possible for your audience to get your message.

In summary, whether you are making a formal presentation before a large audience or a short talk to several people in the office, visual aids can make the job easier. Just be sure you select the proper medium, and keep in mind that it may well be you.

A sardonic remark you often hear is, ''What do you want me to do, draw you a picture?''

The answer is yes! A picture can do the job when words just aren't enough, or when words are too much. Use visuals to do what words can't, or to cut a long, descriptive paragraph into an easily understood graphic. When the going gets tough, don't despair. Draw them a picture!

Room Design

Unfortunately, most conference rooms are not designed by professional speakers. As a result, you will often be stuck with a room that doesn't lend itself to the structure you want to give your presentation.

There are a few basic rules for setting up a room to give you and your visuals an opportunity to have the impact you've worked so hard to achieve. If the room in which you will be speaking has built-in projectors, screens, or chalkboards that don't allow you a choice, consider a different medium or bringing portable equipment.

The most important consideration is to set up the room so that you are at center stage, not your visual. This is where most rooms are disappointing, because the mounted screen or board is usually in the center. This forces you to stand aside and play second fiddle to the visual.

Arrange your screen, board, or easel so that it is slightly to one side and behind you. Be sure that every person can see every visual. When setting up projectors, arrange the room to create an aisle where you need one. Check the arrangement by sitting in a few seats here and there in the audience, being sure that no one is going to be trying to see the screen through the projector.

If you are using both a lectern and visuals, give yourself plenty of room to move around; don't crowd yourself into a small space between the two. You might try placing the lectern at a slight angle and farther to one side. This keeps your notes handy but lets you move freely.

Some visuals are very difficult to use at the same time as a microphone. Think through your entire environment before you decide on what medium to use, and try to have a hand-held or clip-on microphone.

Be sure that you have only enough chairs set out for the expected number of people. If it is a meeting of thirty-five people, don't set up a hundred chairs. This causes the audience to think that everyone else stayed away and wonder why. It is usually better to set up thirty chairs for a meeting of thirty-five people and have extra chairs readily available. Arrange ahead of time for the chairs to be set up the way you want them, with or without an aisle, in straight rows or semicircular, tables or not. Of course, you won't always have control over this, but it doesn't hurt to ask. Most people are willing to adjust their setup habits if they think they will enjoy the presentation more by doing so.

In general, try to set up the room so that you, your audience, and your visuals are "proxemic," or at a pleasing distance from one another. Strive for a sense of closeness without making your audience feel trapped or walked on. Allow yourself enough room to move freely, and your audience enough room to sit comfortably. Following are some examples of how you might set up your speaking environment.

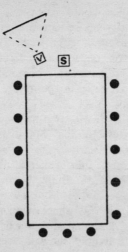

For small groups of up to 12–15 people, a standard conference table works well. This tends to be more formal.

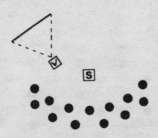

A less formal option for small groups is a semicircular design.

S = Speaker
V = Visual

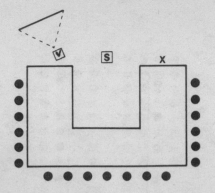

A horseshoe design, or "U" shape, works well for groups of up to 15–20 people. A second projector or flip chart could be placed at the "X." It may show the same visual, or you could alternate between the two.

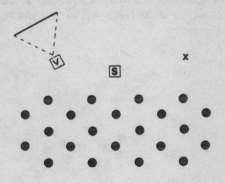

Random seating is appropriate for larger groups. Tables can be added if your audience will need to take notes. In some conference rooms, the screen is attached to the center of the wall; you may need to ask people to move so they can see better. A second visual could be used here as well.

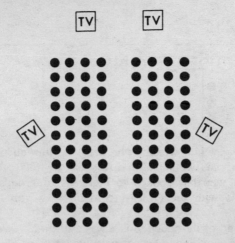

Be sure you arrange for enough monitors for everyone to see clearly. The number of monitors you need will depend on the seating arrangement and the size of the screen. Be sure to place the monitors on stands so that they are slightly above the heads of the audience.

Chapter 15

INTRODUCTIONS

"Our speaker is a woman who needs no introduction . . . a woman who is well qualified to speak on this subject . . . a woman who has spoken to hundreds of groups like our own. It is with great pleasure that I give you Ms. J. J. Jones!"

This kind of introduction is a waste of time.

Is there anything in it to make you believe this speaker will be exciting, different, or challenging? Because we have heard that introduction so many times before, it will be pretty tough for us to not think that we've heard the speech too.

The introduction above serves no purpose whatsoever; it just barely observes the courtesy of having an introduction at all. It is stilted, cliché-ridden, and boring; it reinforces the apathetic attitude of the audience.

At some point in your career, or maybe as part of your involvement with community groups and clubs, you will be called upon to introduce a speaker. So make your introduction a good one!

A good introduction should:

- excite interest in the subject

- excite interest in the speaker

- be brief

- set the right mood

Tips for Introducing a Speaker

An introduction should tell the audience what the subject is, why they should be interested in it, who the speaker is, and what he or she has done to earn the right to address them. But all of this should be "short and sweet": the audience has come to hear the speaker, not the introducer. Following are some helpful guidelines.

Get the speaker's subject straight. Nothing is more disconcerting to a speaker than to have the introducer set up the audience for the wrong speech. Even vagueness on the subject matter is upsetting. Contact the speaker in advance and get all the information you need to be specific about the topic.

Get the audience interested. This is sometimes a challenging task—especially if you feel the speaker may be a poor one. But your job is to make the topic appealing to the audience, and mumbling, "The subject is one of great interest," won't do it. You have to be specific and give a couple of creative examples.

Don't "scoop" the speaker. Use good judgment in determining what you will say to arouse audience interest without stealing the speaker's thunder. You might contact the speaker and ask for a couple of appropriate benefits or examples—but be sure you tell the speaker you are looking for something for the introduction, so there are no surprises for her.

Answer the audience's question, "Who is she?" Name and title are important, but do go beyond them. In one or two sentences, give some details of the speaker's background or accomplishments that particularly qualify her on this topic.

Don't take too much time. Most introductions can be made in less than one minute. Some may demand as much as two. But let the audience get what they came for—the speaker—as soon as possible.

Set the right climate. You can be a real hero with the speaker if you "set up" the audience for her. If your speaker's talk is going to be humorous, you can use a light introduction that sets the mood. Or, in the same situation, you might be very serious and underplay the introduction to set up contrast for the speaker. If the speaker is following another on a totally unrelated topic, you need to make the transition. Your challenge is to sweep the audience's mind clean of the last topic and prepare them for the next.

Be original. Avoid the trite phrases with which this chapter opened. Try for the unusual with imaginative ideas and language. If you find yourself about to say, "We have with us tonight . . ." or "We are indeed fortunate . . ." stop! The audience has heard that a thousand times before. Say instead, "You're going to enjoy Ms. Jones. . . ." or "I was really pleased when Ms. Jones agreed to talk to us. . . ." (They've only been said a few hundred times!) Try meeting the speaker well before the presentation; this may give you the opportunity to make a personal and more effective introduction.

"Brief" the speaker. Aside from being courteous, letting the speaker know beforehand what you are planning to say can save you both a lot of embarrassment. Check the details in your introduction, and be sure you have the facts straight.

In addition, listen to the speaker pronounce her name for you a few times and practice saying it yourself. Then if you get up there and still have trouble with the pronunciation, don't stumble around or let your voice waver; say it any way you can, and sound as if it's right. A good speaker will not correct you but simply pronounce her name correctly somewhere in the presentation. (If this happens when you are speaking, a good way to let the audience know your correct name is to refer to yourself by name during the presentation.)

Don't tell inappropriate jokes. This is a sound warning for any time, but it's especially important in introductions. For some reason an emcee often feels he must tell a few jokes—whether they are relevant or not. Humor may be appropriate, but jokes are not the only form of humor. Some people can find the "right" joke that really ties in with the subject and tell it well. But this is a talent that most of us do not have. Even if you can tell a good joke when you're with friends, it doesn't mean your jokes will come off well in a speaking situation. So treat this form of humor with the respect it deserves and stay away if it isn't your forte.

Be considerate of the speaker. Give her a cue when it's time for her to get up; don't have her rising and falling in her seat like a yo-yo as you think of one more thing to say. Announce her name when you are transferring the floor to her, then move out of her way. Give her your full attention when she begins to speak; don't whisper to someone or check your notes.

When the speaker is through, let her acknowledge the applause before you rise. Then thank her for the talk and make some reference to the content to show you heard it. Don't exaggerate about the quality of the presentation. If the speaker was inspiring, say so. If not, thank her for her time and ideas but say nothing about the quality.

If you now think introducing someone is no small task—you're right. Good introductions require a high degree of imagination, planning, and finesse. To be a success at it, just be yourself, use these tips, and practice.

Writing Your Own Introduction

You can avoid a poor introduction of your next presentation by writing it yourself. Take a few moments to decide what you want the audience to know about you and your topic. Type this up for your introducer, sending a copy ahead of time and taking one with you to the presentation.

Be sure you have a conversation with the emcee so that he

understands why you prefer him to use the introduction you prepared. This won't guarantee that he'll use it, so be prepared to gracefully accept whatever you get. You may have to adjust your first few comments, so be alert and flexible. Following is an example of an introduction.

JANICE J. JONES

Janice Jones has been employed by ABC Manufacturing for more than ten years. In her current position as Vice President of Finance, she is responsible for an annual budget of 950 million dollars.

She has authored many articles appearing in national trade journals and has recently written the book *Manufacturing Money*. Janice will speak today about a difficult issue for many of us: "International Money: A Look Into the Crystal Ball."

This introduction can be read in less than one minute. It establishes credibility for the speaker, yet allows Janice to open her presentation in any number of attention-getting ways. You may wish to use this sample to develop your own introduction.

A FEW FINAL WORDS

Well, there you have it—the keys to communicating effectively with one or many. The increasing importance of communication in our society cannot be overemphasized. A leading management consultant recently said that the single most important activity you will be involved in throughout your life is communication. This has some important implications for both our personal and professional lives. The "high tech–high touch" society that John Naisbitt describes in *Megatrends* is upon us in many ways—the more technical our society becomes, the more we seek face-to-face experiences with one another. The success of these highly important interpersonal relationships will greatly depend on our ability to communicate.

Competition in the job market will become increasingly tougher. In addition, success in any leadership role will depend on your ability to communicate well. Who will be selected? The people that have the appropriate skills, of course. But all things being equal, when push comes to shove, the people who get the jobs will be the ones who can best communicate about themselves and the work they do.

This is the beginning. After reading and studying the principles in this book, you are ready to begin a commitment to a lifetime practice of communicating effectively. Whether you are explaining, persuading, teaching, selling, or sharing ideas, these principles will help you. Combine them with your personal and professional strengths and you will be successful.

This has been proven time and again by the hundreds of people who have completed our course in communication. You've got the basics—now it is up to you to put them into practice whenever you communicate with your coworkers, family, neighbors, and friends. Every opportunity to express yourself is a chance to put these principles into action. Only a few of us will give speeches, but all of us will communicate every day of our lives. Using these principles will help you do it more effectively. We wish you the best of luck as you do so.

—Marcelle A. Brashear
John H. Schaefer

REFERENCES AND SUGGESTED READING

Bartlett, John. *Bartlett's Quotations*. Boston: Little, Brown and Co., 1980 (15th Edition).

Byan, Richard. *Words That Sell*. Westbury, New York: Caddylak Publishing, 1984.

Gallway, Timothy W. *The Inner Game of Tennis*. New York: Bantam, 1974.

Hammond Landau, Jennifer and Jean Westcott. *Field Guide to Flip Charts*. MACAW Desktop Publishing, 1987.

Johnson, Spencer and Larry Wilson. *The One Minute Sales Person*. New York: Avon Books, 1984.

Kafka, Vincent W. and John H. Schaefer. *Open Management*. New York: Peter H. Wyden, 1975.

Mehrabian, Albert. *Silent Messages*. Belmont, CA: Wadsworth Publishing, 1981.

Molcho, Samy. *Body Speech*. New York: St. Martin's Press, 1985.

Osborn, Alex F. *Applied Imagination*. New York: Charles Scribner's Sons, 1963.

Powell, J. Lewis. *Executive Speaking: An Acquired Skill*. Washington, D.C.: BNA Inc., 1972.

Spinrad, Leonard and Thelma. *Speaker's Lifetime Library*. New York: Parker Publishing, 1979.

Tyler, V. Lynn. *Intercultural Interacting*. Provo, Utah: Brigham Young University, 1987.

Waitley, Dr. Denis. *The Psychology of Winning*. New York: Berkley Books, 1984.

Wallenchinsky, David, Irving Wallace, and Amy Wallace. *The Book of Lists*. New York: Bantam Books, 1984.

Zelany, Gene. *Say it With Charts*. Homewood, IL: Dow Jones-Irwin, 1985.

BE A WINNER!
with these books by
DR. DENIS WAITLEY

____**THE DOUBLE WIN** 0-425-08530-9/$3.95
For anyone who has the desire to excel, here's
how to get to the top without putting others down.

____**THE WINNER'S EDGE** 0-425-10000-6/$3.50
How to develop your success potential, by the
man who has made a career of helping others get
ahead.

____**THE PSYCHOLOGY OF WINNING**
0-425-09999-7/$3.95
Learn the ten vital secrets of success--from self-
awareness, to self-projection!

Check book(s). Fill out coupon. Send to:

BERKLEY PUBLISHING GROUP
390 Murray Hill Pkwy., Dept. B
East Rutherford, NJ 07073

NAME_____

ADDRESS_____

CITY_____

STATE_____ZIP_____

**PLEASE ALLOW 6 WEEKS FOR DELIVERY.
PRICES ARE SUBJECT TO CHANGE
WITHOUT NOTICE.**

POSTAGE AND HANDLING:
$1.00 for one book, 25¢ for each ad-
ditional. Do not exceed $3.50.

BOOK TOTAL $____

POSTAGE & HANDLING $____

APPLICABLE SALES TAX $____
(CA, NJ, NY, PA)

TOTAL AMOUNT DUE $____

PAYABLE IN US FUNDS.
(No cash orders accepted.)

240